ngry Smile

The Angry Smile

The Psychology of
Passive-Aggressive Behavior in
Families, Schools, and Workplaces

Second Edition

DISCARD

Jody E. Long

Nicholas J. Long

Signe Whitson

pro·ed
An International Publisher

8700 Shoal Creek Boulevard
Austin, Texas 78757-6897
800/897-3202   Fax 800/397-7633
www.proedinc.com

© 2001, 2009 by PRO-ED, Inc.
8700 Shoal Creek Boulevard
Austin, Texas 78757-6897
800/897-3202   Fax 800/397-7633
www.proedinc.com

Library of Congress Cataloging-in-Publication Data

Long, Jody.
    The angry smile : the psychology of passive-aggressive behavior in families, schools, and workplaces /
Jody E. Long, Nicholas J. Long, and Signe Whitson.—2nd ed.
        p.   cm.
    Previously published as: Long, Nicholas, 1929— Managing passive-aggressive behavior of children and
youth at school and home, © 2001
        ISBN 978-1-4164-0423-1 (alk. paper)
        1. Oppositional defiant disorder in children—Popular works. 2. Oppositional defiant disorder in adoles-
cence—Popular works. 3. Passive-aggressive personality—Popular works.   I. Long, Nicholas James,
1929— II. Whitson, Signe.   III. Long, Nicholas, 1929— Managing passive-aggressive behavior of children and
youth at school and home.   IV. Title.
RJ506.O66L66 2009
618.92'8581—dc22

                                                                                          2008033993

Art Director: Jason Crosier
Designer: Vicki DePountis
This book is designed in Janson Text and Triplex.

Printed in the United States of America
1 2 3 4 5 6 7 8 9 10   17 16 15 14 13 12 11 10 09 08

To our grandchildren, Taylor, Keith, Ryan, Julia, Kara, and Nolan:

May they enjoy the challenge and pleasure of writing

—Jody and Nicholas Long

To Richard, Hannah, and Elle: My three great loves

—Signe Whitson

I was angry with a friend:
I told my wrath, my wrath did end.
I was angry with my foe:
I told it not, my wrath did grow.

William Blake

Contents

PART 3
Changing Passive-Aggressive Behaviors

What Is Passive Aggression?

The Secret World of Passive Aggression

1

Procrastination is a friend of ours. Unfortunately, it also is a behavior of people who are passive aggressive. *The Angry Smile: The Psychology of Passive-Aggressive Behavior in Families, Schools, and Workplaces* was not written on an impulse or on any publisher's deadline. We have been studying the psychology of passive aggression for more than 4 decades as part of our clinical and educational work with troubled youth, anxious professionals, conflicted parents, contradictory spouses, hostile coworkers, and resistant bosses.

Our interest in passive aggression began in 1962, when Nicholas accepted a position as the director of Hillcrest Children's Center, a psychiatric residential treatment program for children and youth with emotional disorders in Washington, DC. We lived on campus and related daily with the students and staff, whom we got to know intimately. The strength of this treatment program was the professional competence of the residential and educational staff and their ability to manage the aggressive and violent outbursts of the troubled children. We often commented on how kind-spirited and therapeutic the staff were and on the high degree of skill they exhibited in controlling their counter-aggressive feelings, particularly when children yelled, cursed, spit, and tried to hit them. It seemed to us that the staff functioned at their very best when the children were behaving at their personal worst. The staff managed to show kindness and tolerance for deviant behavior for all of the children, except for one 12-year-old student named Jason.

Jason was an exceptionally intelligent, attractive, well-groomed, middle-class student who had a perpetual sarcastic smile on his face. Jason never lost his self-control or showed any explosive behaviors. He did not scream or swear at the staff, and at times he was downright pleasant and cooperative. But when Jason made a personal decision not to follow a rule or staff directive, he would quietly and systematically become oppositional, which would frustrate the staff. Jason had the rare diagnostic skill of being able to identify each adult's Achilles' heel, and he purposefully behaved in a way that played on their unique vulnerabilities. One by one, he succeeded in stirring up intense counter-aggressive feelings in each competent staff person. Jason was the student that staff deemed most difficult, and the one they most wanted to punish.

How was it possible that this quiet, bright, preadolescent boy could cause so much frustration and anger within and among a sophisticated staff? We did not have an answer in 1962, but today the answer is obvious: Jason was a troubled boy with a classic passive-aggressive personality.

Because of Jason's patterns of behavior and the staff's unusual reactions to him, we decided to learn more about the dynamics of passive aggression. The psychiatric literature on passive aggression in 1963 was limited. As a result, we developed ongoing seminars on passive-aggressive behavior and invited colleagues, parents, and teachers who were interested in this topic. The only requirement for participation was their willingness to discuss and write up their experiences and observations on passive-aggressive behavior at school and home.

Prior to the first edition of this text in 2001, we conducted more than 50 seminars on passive aggression around the United States and collected over 1,200 personal examples of passive-aggressive behavior in school and at home. As we analyzed these examples, a new and exciting theoretical explanation of passive-aggressive behavior emerged.

In the past 7 years, a new generation of *Angry Smile* seminars has been born, thanks to interest in the book and to our close ties with Life Space Crisis Intervention trainers, who began offering their own series of seminars. A whole new crop of experiences and examples—along with frustrations and emotion—flooded in. The seminar stories convinced us that there was still more of this phenomenon to explore and that any revision of our text would have to include adults as well as children, and workplace scenarios along with those of school and home.

What Motivated Participants to Attend Our Seminars

As we talked with our seminar participants, many of them told us they were curious to know if they were teaching, living, or working with someone who was passive aggressive. The participants also were interested to discover if they were themselves passive aggressive. We said they could get a glimpse of insight by answering these two diagnostic questions:

DIAGNOSTIC QUESTION 1: Is there a person in your life who irritates and frustrates you in insignificant and endless ways, so that over time you have a spontaneous urge to choke this person? If a name comes quickly to mind, the chances are you have identified a person with passive-aggressive behavior.

DIAGNOSTIC QUESTION 2: Do you get pleasure and satisfaction from consciously thwarting and quietly getting back at others? Do you find yourself habitually procrastinating, sulking, forgetting, being intentionally inefficient, plotting hidden revenge, or even spiting yourself just to hurt others? If so, you probably have identified yourself as a person with passive-aggressive behavior.

Once the participants' laughter subsided, we became serious and focused on the complexity of teaching, working, and living with passive-aggressive behavior. We are grateful to the hundreds of graduate students, teachers, parents, and other professionals who participated in these seminars. Without their enthusiastic support and examples, this book never would have been written, and we would still be wondering why Jason was such a frustrating student for all of us.

Lack of Professional Interest

Every aspect of life in the 21st century seems to be studied, reported, and filed onto the World Wide Web. From microanalysis of DNA particles to cosmic evolution, nothing seems too small or too large to escape extensive scientific curiosity and scrutiny. Nothing, that is, except the study of passive aggression.

This bold statement is supported by a current literature search that included the Educational Resource Information Center (ERIC) database and PsycARTICLES. ERIC is the major educational research database of our country. ERIC reviews more than 700 professional educational journals each year for the database. PsycARTICLES, from the American Psychological Association (APA), is a definitive source of full-text, peer-reviewed scholarly and scientific articles in psychology. The database contains more than 100,000 articles from 59 journals.

We ran a literature search on aggression and passive aggression using both databases over a 20-year period, from 1987 to 2007. Because passive-aggressive interactions are so anecdotally common, we assumed we would discover a rich history of studies on such behaviors in schools through the ERIC database. However, from 1987 to 2007, there were 2,796 professional articles and studies on aggression compared to just three articles and studies on passive aggression in schools. Using PsycARTICLES, we found similar results: 772 articles on the topic of aggression, compared to seven articles on passive aggression—only one of which had been published since the turn of this century.

What accounts for this surprising finding? It is certainly not the case that passive aggression is a rare behavioral pattern or that it does not cause legitimate psychological discomfort. Based on our professional experiences, workshops on passive aggression, and daily interactions with the public, we intuitively know that passive-aggressive behavior abounds in our society. Beyond intuition, a 2008 Google search brings up about 270,000 links to passive aggression in 0.09 seconds (compared to 17.5 million links for aggression in less than 1 second). While these Internet links do not carry the weight of scientific study, they do give strong evidence to support the pervasiveness of passive-aggressive behavior and of the millions of laypeople whose frustration with this behavior drives them to seek helpful information.

The obvious conclusion from the literature searches, however, is that the psychological study of passive aggression has eluded widespread professional scrutiny. And really, given its covert nature, perhaps this should be expected. Passive aggression is not the in-your-face force that aggression is, nor is it the immediately debilitating blow of depression. It simmers beneath the surface, settling under the skin of its victims over the long term—ever present, maddening, and most often out of view to the naked eye.

A Brief History of the Mystery of Passive Aggression

The term *passive aggressive* was first coined by army psychiatrist William Menninger during the Second World War. Colonel Menninger noted a troublesome pattern of behavior among soldiers, in which they followed orders but did so with benign disobedience. Coping with strict regimentation and a climate of conformity, soldiers resisted orders or carried them out to the letter of the law—ignoring the spirit of the command completely. They obeyed authority to its face but were ready to turn their backs at the first chance. Menninger labeled soldiers who displayed this pattern of just-below-the-surface hostility as passive aggressive. It has been accepted since then that the military—and any other organization (e.g., school), entity (e.g., family), or workplace that provides limited opportunities for self-expression or personal freedom—is ideal for eliciting passive-aggressive behavior.

The Veterans Administration first began using the label *passive aggression* as a clinical term for its patients. In the first edition of the American Psychiatric Association's *Diagnostic and Statistical Manual of Mental Disorders (DSM)*, published in 1952, the passive-aggressive personality was described. In the editions of the *DSM* that have been published to date, the debate over the true nature and classification of passive aggression is chronicled. First dubbed a personality style with three distinct subtypes, it was changed to a singular style of "hidden hostility" in *DSM-II* (1968), debated as a defense mechanism and almost omitted from the *DSM-III* (1980), classified as Axis II Personality Disorder (though still relegated to Appendix B as an item for further study) in *DSM-IV* (1994), and finally published (in the appendix) as a provisional diagnosis with the added term *negativistic* in the *DSM-IV-TR* (2000) (see Table 1.1).

A rich debate about passive aggression will likely continue, be it with the publication of the *DSM-V* or with our work here. We do know that passive-aggressive behavior is at once puzzling and pervasive. Researchers may differ on its classification, but receivers of passive-aggressive behavior unite in their confusion over what to do, how to respond, and even how to recognize it before relationships are damaged beyond repair.

Confronting History's Mystery

The Angry Smile: The Psychology of Passive-Aggressive Behavior in Families, Schools, and Workplaces offers a road map for effectively navigating the convoluted and obstacle-laden pathways of engagement with a passive-aggressive person.

School

For schoolteachers, aides, administrators, and crisis counselors who, from September to May, feel their professional skills being chipped away daily by a charming but manipulative student, we offer relatable examples and practical strategies for reclaiming their classrooms.

Home

For mothers, fathers, grandparents, and caretakers of children who procrastinate, "forget," blame others, avoid responsibility, and win by losing as a way of life, this book will shed light on how these patterns have formed and what can be done to alter them.

Table 1.1

Passive-Aggressive Personality Disorder Features

The essential feature [of passive-aggressive personality disorder] is a pervasive pattern of negativistic attitudes and passive resistance to demands for adequate performance in social and occupational situations that begins by early adulthood and that occurs in a variety of contexts. This pattern does not occur exclusively during Major Depressive Episodes and is not better accounted for by Dysthymic Disorder. These individuals habitually resent, oppose, and resist demands to function at a level expected by others. This opposition occurs most frequently in work situations but can also be evident in social functioning. The resistance is expressed by procrastination, forgetfulness, stubbornness, and intentional inefficiency, especially in response to tasks assigned by authority figures. These individuals obstruct the efforts of others by failing to do their share of the work. For example, when an executive gives a subordinate some material to review for a meeting the next morning, the subordinate may misplace or misfile the material rather than point out that there is insufficient time to do the work. These individuals feel cheated, unappreciated, and misunderstood and chronically complain to others. When difficulties appear, they blame their failures on the behaviors of others. They may be sullen, irritable, impatient, argumentative, cynical, skeptical, and contrary. Authority figures (e.g., a superior at work, a teacher at school, a parent, or a spouse who acts the role of a parent) often become the focus of discontent. Because of their negativism and tendency to externalize blame, these individuals often criticize and voice hostility toward authority figures with minimal provocation. They are also envious and resentful of peers who succeed or who are viewed positively by authority figures. These individuals often complain about their personal misfortunes. They have a negative view of the future and may make comments such as, "It doesn't pay to be good" and "Good things don't last." These individuals may waver between expressing hostile defiance toward those they view as causing their problems and attempting to mollify these persons by asking forgiveness or promising to perform better in the future.

Associated Features

These individuals are often overtly ambivalent, wavering indecisively from one course of action to its opposite. They may follow an erratic path that causes endless wrangles with others and disappointments for themselves. An intense conflict between dependence on others and the desire for self-assertion is characteristic of these individuals. Their self-confidence is often poor despite a superficial bravado. They foresee the worst possible outcome for most situations, even those that are going well. This defeatist outlook can evoke hostile and negative responses from others who are subjected to the complaints of these individuals. This pattern of behavior often occurs in individuals with Borderline, Histrionic, Paranoid, Dependent, Antisocial, and Avoidant Personality Disorders.

Note. From *Diagnostic and Statistical Manual of Mental Disorders–Fourth Edition–Text Revision* (pp. 789–790), 2000, Washington, DC: American Psychiatric Association. Copyright 2000 by American Psychiatric Association. Reprinted with permission.

Close Adult Relationships

For adult children of passive-aggressive parents, husbands, wives, boyfriends, girlfriends, best friends, and anyone involved in a relationship with an often sullen, bitingly sarcastic, resentful, endless excuse-making person who shuts down openly hostile discussions by turning up the stereo or muttering, "Fine" from behind his newspaper, we will show you how to modulate your own emotional responses to and turn down the heat of a passive-aggressive conflict.

Workplace

And for those both high and low on the office food chain—employees and bosses who are at the receiving end of intentionally inefficient work, frequent hard drive crashes, late arrivals, conveniently timed sick days, nasty (and endless) e-mail exchanges, and hidden agendas, *The Angry Smile* offers techniques for stopping the perfect office crimes of passive aggression.

Skills You Will Learn

In the pages that follow, you will

1. come to understand the development of passive-aggressive behavior, from its childhood origins to its troublesome manifestations in school, at home, in close adult relationships, and in the workplace;

2. increase your awareness of the reasons why people of all ages use passive-aggressive behaviors and distinguish between situational and pathological passive aggression;

3. examine five distinct levels of passive-aggressive behavior and recognize how behavior in school, home, and the workplace falls within these levels; and

4. come to understand the Passive-Aggressive Conflict Cycle, our paradigm for explaining the circular and escalating behavior between a passive-aggressive person and his or her unsuspecting target.

We know that anyone who picks up a book such as ours has an intellectual thirst for theory but also a practical hunger for answering the question, "Now, what do I *do*?" What makes *The Angry Smile* so valuable is the cognitive road map it provides for not only understanding the nature of passive-aggressive behavior but also effectively confronting it. To challenge passive resistance, you will learn to use the following:

- The 5-step process of Benign Confrontation with children and adults, in school, at home, in close adult relationships, and in the workplace. Through real-world examples, we will show you how Benign Confrontation can be used effectively at all five levels of passive-aggressive behavior.

- Skills for recognizing the red flags of passive-aggressive behavior. Those who become adept at recognizing this troubling pattern early on do not get caught up in the Passive-Aggressive Conflict Cycle, which jeopardizes academic success, damages relationships, and brings down careers. For easy reference, we will provide symptom checklists and important intervention notes throughout the text.

The Need to Clarify Psychological Terms

Any attempt to bring the dynamics of passive aggression to the surface needs to begin with a clarification of related terms and concepts. Unfortunately, there is ample psychobabble in popular literature regarding emotional and behavioral terms. Pop psychology distorts the importance of meaningful psychological terms and significant diagnostic distinctions. Before moving further with our findings, we present the following psychological definitions in an effort to clear away ambiguity and sharpen our focus on the study of passive aggression.

Anger

Anger is a basic, spontaneous, temporary, internalized, neurophysiological *feeling* usually triggered by frustration and consciously experienced as an unpleasant personal state. Anger ebbs and flows in our daily lives. It is a real, powerful, and natural emotion, but it does not always reflect an accurate perception of the precipitating event.

> Rebecca was angry at her father for making her fold the laundry. Following his request, she angrily yelled, "You make me do everything around here!" She slammed the dryer closed and stormed out of the room.

Aggression

Aggression is one way the feeling of anger is expressed in *behavior*. Aggression usually is a spontaneous and unplanned act. It often takes the form of an impulsive action. Aggressive behavior is destructive because it aims to depreciate, hurt, or destroy a person or an object. Aggression can be an automatic response to mounting pain and anxiety that is expressed by yelling, cursing, threatening, or hitting others.

> Al is a supervisor with a reputation for getting the job done. He delegated a large assignment to novice worker Katherine, who failed to turn the work in on time. When the responsibility was placed on his shoulders during a quarterly interdepartmental meeting, Al stood up at his seat and was verbally aggressive to Katherine, cursing her skills, lambasting her intelligence, and suggesting that she be fired on the spot.

Hate

Hate is a focused or laser-beam *feeling* of anger. Hate is a feeling that has a specific target in mind. It is most often triggered by feelings of embarrassment, revenge, and prejudice. Hate is like frozen anger that rarely melts. Hate can be learned and passed on from one generation to the next. Hate can take the form of personal, racial, national, religious, political, or familial hatred.

> In algebra class, Mrs. Ross called on Michael to go to the blackboard to demonstrate the solution to an equation. Michael struggled with math and was intensely uncomfortable standing up in front of his peers. He believed Mrs. Ross knew this! His entirely body stiffened, he clenched his fists, and he felt hatred toward his perceived ruthless teacher.

Hostility

Hostility is a conscious and deliberate *behavior* motivated by hate and intended to depreciate, hurt, or destroy a person or object. Unlike aggression, the act of hostility does not have to occur immediately or impulsively; it can take place a day, a week, a month, or even a year later. Hostility is a personal vendetta often motivated by revenge.

> Alicia expected to get a high-profile promotion at work. Her boss had done everything but hand her the new job description. When a less experienced colleague got the promotion instead, Alicia felt professionally humiliated. For the next 6 months, both her boss and the promoted coworker felt the full force of Alicia's hostility. From open acts of sabotage to behind-the-scenes work obstructions, Alicia let her emotion be known.

Rage

Rage is the runaway *feeling* of anger or hate. Rage is the primitive beast within us, which erupts whenever we feel helpless. A rage reaction usually occurs when a person's coping skills are stripped away and the person has no other way of responding to what he or she perceives as an overwhelming situation of psychological or physical threat.

> Six-year-old Benjamin is repeatedly abused by a family member. He feels defenseless to stop the abuse and believes his parents know about it and are failing to protect him. Frightened of the abuser, Benjamin does nothing to fight back during his childhood but carries with him into adulthood a righteous rage. During periods of high stress or even in routine interactions, when thoughts of his abuse are inadvertently triggered, his rage erupts onto unsuspecting and undeserving others.

Violence

Violence is the destructive *behavior* through which a person expresses intense feelings of anger and hate that have turned into rage. Violence is like a volcano. It does not target any person. It is out-of-control behavior that erupts and injures everyone in its path. Very often, the victims of violence just happen to be in the wrong place at the wrong time.

> Samantha and Miguel have a stormy marriage. When times are good, they say they are deeply in love and committed to their marriage. However, when arguments break out—and they often do—a pattern of domestic violence emerges. Both partners express their anger and rage by throwing heavy items, punching walls, pushing each other, and screaming at their children.

Passivity

The passive person communicates his or her needs, wants, and feelings in an indirect, emotionally dishonest way. Through passive *behaviors*, passive individuals allow their own rights to be violated because of their personal belief that their needs are not worthy of consideration or that their feelings are not as important as those of others. Passive behavior may take the form of poor eye contact or hesitant speech and often results in the passive person feeling even greater anxiety, helplessness, and internalized anger.

> Tasha is bullied by her classmate, Blair. She is pushed, publicly ridiculed, and often excluded from peer group events. Tasha's parents have encouraged her to assertively stand up for herself by making the teacher aware of the situation or by telling Blair to "knock it off." Instead, Tasha's passive nature prevails. When her teacher tries to help, Tasha waves her off saying, "I don't mind." She answers Blair's shoves with offers to do the tormentor's homework. Through such actions, she conveys the clear message: "Tease me again. I won't stand up for myself, and I'll even come back for more because what I want most is to be accepted by you."

Counter Aggression

Counter-aggressive *behaviors* are the common cold of the anger world. They occur when a nonaggressive person interacts with other people who are aggressive or hostile and, in a sense, "catches" their anger, as they would an airborne disease. By acting on counter-aggressive feelings, the normally "healthy" person mirrors the behaviors of the person who had the original anger bug. Both end up behaving badly.

> Mrs. Davis asks the class to sit down in their seats. Everyone sits but Zachary, who looks her straight in the eye and says, "You can't make me!" Mrs. Davis stands up at her own desk and repeats her instruction in a slightly raised voice.
> "I said *no!*" Zachary replied loudly.
> "If you want to be a troublemaker, then you can stand all day, Michael," she yells, marching over to his seat and taking his chair back to her desk at the front of the classroom.

Counter-aggressive behaviors can be identified because they are based on "you" messages:

> "You make me mad."

> "You are always so incompetent."

> "You better apologize."

> "You never use your head."

Counter-aggressive behavior usually attacks the personality of the other person and guarantees that interpersonal conflict will escalate.

Assertiveness

Assertiveness is learned *behavior* that is used to express anger in a verbal, nonblaming, respectful way. Assertive behavior clearly sets the limits of what a person is willing to do or not do in an interpersonal situation. Unlike passivity and aggression, assertive behavior does not depreciate or cause harm to either person. It is a healthy way of defining the boundaries of one's personal reality.

Assertive behavior is an effective way of making friends with one's personal anger so that behavior becomes constructive rather than destructive. In contrast to counter aggression, assertiveness is based on using "I" messages:

"I want to share with you that I am having difficulty dealing with your lateness. I become irritated when you promise to meet me at noon but are late. Three times this week I have had to wait for you for at least 30 minutes."

Very often, when a passive person is learning to communicate emotion more effectively, he or she first swings too far to the aggressive side, and when the aggressive person is first attempting to tone down his or her emotional rhetoric, he or she errs on the side of passivity. Assertiveness is the essential middle ground between the ineffective communication extremes of passivity and aggression. Its ideal situation in the center, however, should not cause it to be confused with passive aggression, which we will examine next.

Passive Aggression

Call it *hostile cooperation*, *sugarcoated hostility*, or *compliant defiance*. Call it all of the above. Along with these synonymous phrases, the term *passive aggression* is an oxymoron. Passive-aggressive behavior does not alternate between passive behavior and aggressive behavior, but rather combines them simultaneously into one behavior that is both confounding and irritating to others.

Passive-aggressive behavior exists in all civilized cultures and at every socioeconomic level. It is a deliberate and masked way of expressing covert feelings of anger. Passive aggression involves a variety of behaviors designed to get back at another person without the other recognizing the underlying anger. In the long run, passive aggression is even more destructive to interpersonal relationships than is aggression, and, over time, all relationships with a person who is passive aggressive will become confusing, discouraging, and dysfunctional.

Passive aggression is motivated by a person's fear of expressing anger directly. The passive-aggressive person believes life will only get worse if other people know of his anger, so he expresses anger indirectly. The passive-aggressive teenager might veil anger by smiling and saying, "Hey, Dad, no problem about not letting me use the car tonight. It's no big deal. I'll call Cindy and see if she'll go out with me another Saturday night." Inside, the teen seethes with anger and plans to make sure his father can't locate his car keys before his Monday morning business meeting. The passive-aggressive spouse who doesn't want to be bothered with household chores might conceal her anger by saying, "I'll do it in a minute" and then waiting so long that her spouse does the chore. Her response when confronted is feigned shock along the lines of, "I didn't know you wanted me to get it done immediately."

We believe the passive-aggressive person derives genuine secondary pleasure out of frustrating others. For this reason, we call this pattern of behavior "the angry smile." Regardless of the term used, people who are passive aggressive often

- deny or repress feelings of anger;

- withdraw and sulk;

- send hidden, coded, and confused messages when frustrated;

- create minor but chronic irritation in others;

- are overtly cooperative but covertly uncooperative;

- procrastinate or carry out tasks inefficiently;

- can be evasive and secretive;

- project angry feelings on others;

- are quietly manipulative and controlling;

- create a feeling in others of being on an emotional roller coaster;

- cause others to swallow their anger and eventually blow up; and

- make endless promises to change.

Counter–Passive Aggression

When reacting to aggression, a person may behave in a counter-aggressive way. When reacting to hostility, a person may behave in a counter-hostile way. Likewise, when reacting to passive aggression, a person may behave in a counter–passive-aggressive way. In Chapter 10, we will present the Passive-Aggressive Conflict Cycle and explain in detail the dynamics of how persons responding to passive aggression frequently end up mirroring the troublesome behavior and getting caught in a circular and endless cycle of passive-aggressive conflict.

> A mother becomes impatient with her son's passive-aggressive pattern of "missing" the bus so that he can use the family car to drive himself to school. On the morning of an important soccer tournament, she "forgets" to wake him on time so that he is late and not able to meet his team in time for the game.

Like atomic waste, counter-aggressive, counter-hostile, and counter–passive-aggressive behaviors are all toxic. Unless a person learns to manage and dispose of these behaviors in a healthy way, he or she will end up contaminating his or her well-being.

A Positive Outcome

As we taught our theory of passive aggression to seminar parents and professionals, we were gratified by their quick insight into the psychology of passive aggression and their sense of personal empowerment to deal with passive-aggressive behaviors. These empowered adults no longer felt like confused victims but acquired the psychological awareness and skills to alter their responses to passive aggression. Many participants commented that their lives became less emotional and more stable. They reported that they were able to identify the anger behind another person's passive-aggressive behavior. Most important, the participants were no longer programmed to fulfill the other person's irrational belief that adults and authority figures are critical, demanding, and at times out of control. We believe you will experience these same feelings of insight and empowerment as you read this book.

Developmental Pathways to a Passive-Aggressive Personality

As we talked with adults who have passive-aggressive personalities, they described their developmental histories in detail. From these interviews, four different socializing life experiences emerged that seemed to explain why they developed passive-aggressive personalities:

Pathway 1: as a reaction to early, prolonged, and excessive psychological and physical parental abuse

Pathway 2: as a reaction to early, prolonged, and excessive parental standards of goodness, social approval, and guilt

Pathway 3: as a reaction to dysfunctional and triangular family dynamics

Pathway 4: as a reaction to disabling conditions and failed expectations

Pathway 1: Reaction to Early, Prolonged, and Excessive Parental Abuse

There is an assumption that the home is a child's primary source of security, nurturing, and protection. Home is the place where parents teach their children a sense of belonging and trust, independence, self-confidence, competence, and altruism. However, for many children, their homes are not protective environments at all but rather are emotional nightmares.

Violence in the United States occurs most often not the street but in the home. According to national child abuse statistics, there are 3 million reports of child abuse—that is, one every 10 seconds—made in the United States each year. Experts estimate that the actual number of incidents of violence against children is three times greater than what is even reported! Domestic violence and child abuse are primary sources of aggression in our society and include physical, psychological, and sexual abuse. This violence occurs at all socioeconomic levels, across ethnic and cultural lines, within all religions, and at all levels of education.

When trusted adults lose control and act in primitive, aggressive ways, a chronic state of anxiety and fear develops in their children. Persistent exposure to domestic violence predisposes children to psychiatric illness. According to Childhelp, 80% of young adults who were abused as children met the diagnostic criteria for at least one psychiatric disorder by the age of 21 (Childhelp, n.d.).

In our work over the past 4 decades, severely emotionally disturbed children and youth have shared with us their experiences and fears of aggression and abuse at home. We provide a few of their painful stories here.

Twelve-Year-Old Tyrone

Tyrone told us how he had observed his alcoholic father beating up his mother to the point where she was bleeding and pleading for him to stop. Afterward, the father took Tyrone into his bedroom and made Tyrone promise he would never tell anyone about what he had seen. The father said this was a private family secret, and he would cut off Tyrone's genitals if he broke this code of silence.

Nine-Year-Old Misty

Misty reported she was forced to get on her knees and kneel in a corner for 3 hours to repent for swearing at her brother. Her parents said this was an evil deed that needed to be punished. Misty reported that this type of punishment happened frequently in her home.

Eleven-Year-Old Cyril

Cyril reported that his mother was high on drugs and in "one of her crazy and frightening rages" when she cut up his clothes. This was his punishment for not picking up his room on time.

Thirteen-Year-Old Erica

Erica revealed to her social worker that her mother's boyfriend repeatedly fondled and kissed her whenever he found her home alone. Last week, when her mother was shopping, he took her to the basement cot and raped her.

These are only a snapshot of the cases in which children experience traumatic abuse by their parents or other adults within their homes. As abused children grow into adulthood, their pathways diverge.

Some youth who experience firsthand the aggressive and unpredictable behavior of authority figures learn to identify with their aggressor and become aggressive youth and criminally violent adults. National statistics indicate that children who experience abuse are 59% more likely to be arrested as a juvenile, 28% more likely to be arrested as an adult, and 30% more likely to commit violent crime. The cycle of abuse is self-perpetuating; it is estimated that one out of every three children who is abused and neglected will abuse his or her own child in the future (Childhelp, n.d.).

Others remain victims throughout their lifetime, inadvertently recreating the violence they experienced as children by marrying violent spouses and becoming victims again. While outside observers question this pattern, survivors of abuse answer the call of the familiar. Their shattered self-esteem does not allow them the belief or feeling that they deserve different or better.

Still others take a more indirect pathway to survival through their volatile, hostile world; they develop a passive-aggressive personality. Just as a child learns not to put his hands on a hot stove, so many traumatized children learn not to express their angry feelings aloud to hostile adults. These children realize quickly that if they show their anger or retaliate, this will lead to further, more intensive punishment. They recognize their feelings of helplessness and lack of power with their dangerous parents.

For children on this developmental pathway, the psychological truism that *nothing grows stronger or becomes more powerful than an unexpressed hostile thought toward others over time* prevails. Rather than run the risk of verbalizing or acting out their anger directly and immediately, these children learn to control and suppress their counter-aggressive feelings toward hurtful adults. While an adept survival skill, this sophisticated ability fuels their hostile thoughts over time. They often think to themselves:

- "I can't get back at you now, but I will find a way. When I do, you won't even know about it."

- "You may think I am subservient and your victim, but I will use all of my intelligence to get back at you."

- "You will regret treating me this way. I will have my revenge, and I will enjoy every minute of it."

Many abused, deprived, and exploited children find passive aggression to be a most successful and satisfying means of survival as they grow up with angry and hostile adults. Unfortunately, this pattern of reacting to aggressive adults frequently spills over to others, independent of their behavior. Once a passive-aggressive youth perceives an authority figure as hostile, regardless of whether the perception is accurate or not, he will react as if the adult were being abusive. Throughout childhood and adolescence, the youth reenacts these patterns at home and in school. As he grows into adulthood, he frequently continues this now well-ingrained passive-aggressive personality pattern in his family, marriage, and workplace relationships.

> Once a passive-aggressive youth perceives an authority figure as hostile, regardless of whether the perception is accurate or not, he will react as if the adult were being abusive.

Pathway 2: Reaction to Early, Prolonged, and Unrealistic Parental Standards and Expectations

A second pattern of early life experiences that promotes the development of a passive-aggressive personality may seem paradoxical because this pattern involves caring, involved parents who love their children and genuinely strive for them to be socially and professionally successful. These parents want their children to be well-behaved and accepted by friends, teachers, and future employers. They want their children to be mature, charming, and well-mannered in all situations. They believe good behavior will enhance their children's chances to make good grades, develop important friendships, win scholarships, and attain a successful professional career.

You may be wondering, "What's so wrong with that? Aren't these reasonable goals that most good parents have for their children?" The distinction is in the degree to which good behavior in children is tied to the child's (and thus the parent's) innate goodness.

Parents who are excessively driven by cultural norms, strong religious beliefs, a high need for social approval, or an urgent desire for their children to benefit from their hard work and financial sacrifices may unwittingly impose unrealistic standards about what it takes to be "good" and therefore set unreasonable expectations of a child's emotional experiences.

Eve was raised in a southern family that enjoyed high social standing but a much lower income level than other members of their exclusive circle. Her parents, ever conscious of this financial inequity, felt intense pressure to exude social superiority in all other forms. The upbringing of Eve became their most high profile manner of demonstrating their worthiness within their social circle.

From an early age, it was made absolutely clear in Eve's family that good children never yelled, spoke, or even thought in negative terms. She learned that good children had pleasant thoughts and behaviors. She was told that good children were never hostile, sarcastic, or ill-mannered. Eve was taught that good children are always nice, cooperative, obedient, and never, ever angry.

As noted in Chapter 1, *anger* is a real, natural emotion. It is basic and spontaneous. It is a neurophysiological feeling. Anger is part of the human condition and, as such, it is neither good nor bad. It just *is*.

Eve's parents enjoyed lavish praise from their friends whenever Eve displayed proper behavior. This confirmed their belief that good behavior = good child = good parent, which was exactly the type of social confirmation they spent their lives seeking. Not only did this equation deny the reality of Eve's human emotion and her normal development, but it also drove her parents to fear the reverse: bad behavior = bad child = bad parent.

Driven by their rigid social structure and upwardly mobile ambitions, Eve's parents equated angry feelings with badness. Rather than separating the natural, human experience of anger from the learned behavior of aggression or violence, they felt it was their parental duty to spend endless hours teaching Eve to suppress her angry feelings.

For children raised in an environment like Eve's, anger becomes a taboo feeling. Parents such as hers are effective not only at inhibiting their children's angry feelings and aggressive behaviors but also at teaching them that even their angry *thoughts* must be controlled. Children are raised with the unrealistic expectation that they must not even *experience* the emotion of anger—in thought, feeling, or deed. If they do, they feel intense guilt about it. The parents are not malicious, but their process of developing proper and well-behaved children is a grievous form of mind control.

Because of her parents' denial that angry thoughts and feelings could even exist, Eve grew up with no direction or options for how to cope with or effectively communicate this most basic human emotion. Though it can be denied, anger can not be abolished; it will persist in all human beings, and for "good" children like

Eve, whose pathways for direct emotional venting are blocked, alternate, indirect channels will be found. Well-intentioned parents like Eve's are unaware of how their over-involvement in promoting goodness in their children will encourage the development of passive-aggressive personalities.

Results of This Socialization

Early, prolonged, and excessive socialization around values of goodness, social acceptance, and guilt encourages a child to hide anger by expressing it indirectly in the following three ways.

1. *Psychosomatic*: The child learns to express anger by swallowing it (see Figure 2.1). One way of expressing anger is to swallow or withdraw from it. This often results in psychosomatic illnesses such as headaches, fatigue, and ulcers, and is captured by the old medical saying, "When you swallow anger, your stomach keeps count." For example, when Eve becomes angry, she is likely to become physically ill and to avoid confrontation by withdrawing from stressful social situations.

2. *Projection*: The child learns to express anger by blaming others (see Figure 2.2). Because Eve is unable to acknowledge or feel comfortable with her anger, she may instead attribute it to others in her world. It is easier for Eve to internalize the belief and say, "This is an angry world and people out there aren't nice to me. They are jealous and mean to me." Instead of saying "I am angry," she projects those feelings onto others and says, "Those kids are really angry, mean, and nasty. Those kids want to fight with me. Those kids must be really bad." Psychologically, Eve attributes to others what she is feeling. During social situations she misreads reality and behaves in a way that encourages her peers, teachers, and others to be aggressive toward her, fulfilling her prophecy that "this is an angry world."

Figure 2.1. Psychosomatic.

Figure 2.2. Projection.

3. *The angry smile*: The child learns to express anger by developing a passive-aggressive personality (see Figure 2.3). The socializing forces of a Pathway 2 passive-aggressive personality are based on adult-imposed standards of goodness, social approval, and guilt about having angry thoughts. Just as rushing waters demand space to flow, so Eve's anger—like that of any human being—will persist until it finds an outlet. Like water, when anger is dammed up, it grows in power. As children like Eve develop into adolescence and adulthood, the force of their passive aggression steadily increases and ultimately has the power to flood academic, family, personal, and professional relationships.

Pathway 3: Reaction to Dysfunctional and Triangular Family Dynamics

The third type of passive-aggressive personality develops from the dynamics of a dysfunctional, triangular family. Although these families may differ in age, background, and tolerance for each other, the parents commonly are upwardly striving middle-class professionals who assume destructive interpersonal roles. Here, we present two variations of problematic family triangles.

Figure 2.3. The angry smile.

A Note About the Healthy Socialization of Anger

There is no debate about the need to control aggressive behavior in children. Parents need to teach children to give up aggressive behaviors that are triggered by angry feelings. Parents need to teach children not to bite, hit, spit, yell, or run away. Children need to develop internal controls over their aggressive impulses, drives, and needs. However, what happens now is more complex. The goal of healthy socialization is to teach children nonhurtful ways of expressing angry feelings while also acknowledging that their angry feelings are a normal part of life and can be expressed through words and natural activities such as climbing, play-acting, painting, and games. Specifically, children need to learn to say yes to the existence of their angry feelings and to say no to the expression of those angry feelings in hurtful and destructive ways. This form of socialization allows the child to live in both worlds: the external world of reality and the internal world of thoughts and feelings.

> Children need to learn to say "yes" to the existence of their angry feelings and to say "no" to the expression of those angry feelings in hurtful and destructive ways.

Variation 1: Dominant Father, Subservient Mother, Passive-Aggressive Child

The first variation consists of a successful, demanding father, a mother who is subservient but angry, and a son who becomes a passive-aggressive personality over years of carrying out his mother's wishes in a passive-aggressive, self-destructive way:

Thomas is a hard-driving, well-educated, successful Type A personality. He is well organized and handles both multiple responsibilities and stressful situations with ease. Thomas is a self-directed man, motivated by the results of his efforts. He is extremely intelligent and skilled socially. In all areas of his life, Thomas sets very high expectations for himself and for those around him. Professionally, he is a success and his colleagues perceive him as competent. His relationships with his family members, however, are marginal. The family does not lack material resources, but many emotional needs remain unfilled. Thomas tends to be unhappy with his marriage because he perceives his wife as being too passive and dependent.

Debby is bright, attractive, quiet, and subservient to Thomas. She does not have an independent career, although she does have a college degree. Debby's self-esteem suffers, and she is viewed as socially reticent. She is unhappy with her marriage because of the pressure Thomas creates in the family. Debby reports that there is too much stress in their lives, and she finds it impossible to keep up with all of her responsibilities. She relates to Thomas by being passive aggressive and nonconfrontational. Moreover, Debby is a closet drinker. This is her way to escape from the loneliness and frustration of her marriage.

Adam is a bright, perceptive teenager who is overvalued by both Thomas and Debby. He is self-centered and narcissistic, seeing himself as intelligent and in competition with his father. Adam is emotionally involved in supporting and defending his mother, whom he feels is unnecessarily depreciated by his father. Without any verbal discussion, an emotional contract develops between the mother and son. Adam agrees to take on and get back at his powerful father by becoming passive aggressive and self-destructive. He knows exactly what the father values and expects of him, so he systematically frustrates his dad in these valued areas.

Though Adam is academically gifted, he fails his high school geometry class because he refuses to complete an assignment on time. At home, Adam tells his father that the work is too "stupid" and to do it would be an insult to his intelligence. Thomas becomes angry and irately expresses his concern that Adam will never get into the "correct" college if he continues to refuse schoolwork and to fail classes. Thomas's anger only feeds his son's resistance. Adam says he is not interested in college and ridicules every attempt to encourage him to attend. Adam knows well that this is a particularly emotional button to press for his father, who values education so highly.

In addition, Adam frequently chooses to dress in a trendy, cult-like style that irritates and embarrasses his father. He sports multicolored hair, uses drugs, and participates in an unusual spiritual group. Adam's arrogant demeanor cries, "I don't care. Nothing is important to me." This is especially true in activities in which his father wants him to be successful. Over the years, Adam becomes a master of excuses, unkept promises, and disguised insults toward his father.

This family's pattern is typical of families with dysfunctional, triangular dynamics. They experience endless conflicts in which the dominant parent often ultimately explodes in enraged confusion at the passive-aggressive child over and over and over again. There are no winners in this triangular family dynamic.

Variation 2: Domineering Mother, Backseat Father, Passive-Aggressive Child

The second variation of a dysfunctional triangular family dynamic is described by psychologist Scott Wetzler (1992a) in *Living With the Passive Aggressive Man: Coping With Hidden Aggression From the Bedroom to the Boardroom*. In this alternate pathway to passive aggression, Wetzler says the mother typically plays the domineering role, compared to a more distant and often devalued role played by the father. Children growing up within this type of dynamic feel over-controlled by their mothers, who set unrealistic expectations and exert undue influence over every aspect of their life. In this family dynamic, the father takes a backseat to the mother and is often devalued by her. As such, the child cannot look to him as a primary role model. Heavily dependent on the mother, the child then grows up wanting her attention and good favor but also resenting her constant incursions.

> Stanhope's earliest memories are of his mother "butting in where she didn't belong." He recalls an incident from first grade in which he asked his teacher to call him "Stan." He did not want to be teased about his full name, as he had been in kindergarten. When she found out about this, Stan's mother came into his classroom and insisted, in front of the teacher and all of his classmates, that his proper first name be used. She then did this at the beginning of every school year until Stanhope reached high school.
>
> From this very day in elementary school, Stan's life became a series of behaviors that would garner her approval but anger her at the same time. To school, he wore the too-dressy clothing that she picked out for him, but he "accidentally" ripped holes in them. He played golf instead of football, per his mother's wishes, but "lost" his expensive clubs and "forgot" about practice until he was dismissed from the team. As a teenager, Stan attended prep school but had several embarrassing suspensions. Likewise, he enrolled in college but dropped out after only one semester.
>
> As an adult, Stan replayed this pattern in all of his significant relationships. With teachers, in romantic relationships, and even at work, he made a lifetime of compliant defiance.

Both variations of the dynamics of triangular families are based on the child who carries a passive-aggressive message to the targeted dominant parent with such determination that the child is willing to sabotage his own life to succeed. The conflict is one of power, based on winning. In the end, however, there are no winners in this dysfunctional dynamic, because everyone in the family loses.

Pathway 4: Reaction to a Disabling Condition and Failed Expectations

According to Smith (1992), students with disabilities may learn to wear many psychological masks to protect themselves from feelings of inadequacy at home, fear and humiliation related to school failure, and peer rejection. Some solve this problem by hiding behind masks of aggression, dependency, or depression. Others discover the psychological advantages of becoming passive aggressive. They soon recognize how effective passive-aggressive behavior is in manipulating and controlling adults. This behavior gives them a sense of power to replace their feelings of inadequacy and allows them to be cleverly oppositional without others recognizing the depth of their underlying anger. Like Jason, described in Chapter 1, students with disabilities who develop a passive-aggressive style can be the most frustrating and difficult to teach and help.

Based on our years of clinical and educational work with passive-aggressive students and hundreds of conversations with directors and principals of special education programs, we believe that children with disabilities are more likely to develop a passive-aggressive personality than other children. More important, teachers, professionals, and parents attending our seminars continue to validate the relationship between some students with disabilities and the development of a passive-aggressive personality. Like Archimedes, who shouted, "Eureka, now I understand!" our participants have made comments such as the following:

> "Now I understand why I am having such an irritating and discouraging time with Susan. Now her passive-aggressive behavior makes sense to me!"

These substantiating comments do not represent hard research data, but they do provide a groundswell of reality support for our Pathway 4 passive-aggressive personality.

A Word of Caution About Labeling

Before we present a psychological rationale for the relationship between disabilities and passive-aggressive personality development, a word of caution is warranted. There is considerable professional concern regarding the negative impact of labeling students according to their disability. The prevailing justification is that these categories are necessary in order to fund special education programs. This may be true, but labeling also promotes negative stereotypical thinking about these students.

Table 2.1 lists the number and percentage of special education students served in federally supported programs by disability type for selected school years from 1976–77 through 2005–06. Any attempt to make sweeping generalizations about these students with disabilities would be naïve and inappropriate. Within each of the 14 categories, the degree of disability varies along a continuum from mild to severe. In addition, these students vary in their ability to accept and cope with their disabilities. Moreover, many students may be included in multiple categories or have additional but undiagnosed disabilities. For example, a student with a specific learning disability may also have a behavior disorder and speech impairment, or a student with a speech impairment may have a learning problem and a physical disability. We believe there are more differences among the students in each category than there are differences between the categories themselves. When it comes to examining the behavior of students with disabilities, again, they differ significantly in the frequency, intensity, and duration of their behaviors. Consequently, we must

(*text continues on p. 28*)

Table 2.1

Children 3 to 21 Years Old Served in Federally Supported Programs for Individuals With Disabilities, by Type of Disability: Selected Years, 1976-77 through 2005-06

Type of disability	1976-77	1980-81	1990-91	1994-95	1995-96	1996-97	1997-98	1998-99	1999-2000	2000-01	2001-02	2002-03	2003-04	2004-05	2005-06
1	2	3	4	5	6	7	8	9	10	11	12	13	14	15	16
Number served (in thousands)															
All disabilities	3,694	4,144	4,710	5,378	5,572	5,737	5,908	6,056	6,195	6,296	6,407	6,523	6,634	6,719	6,713
Specific learning disabilities	796	1,462	2,129	2,489	2,578	2,651	2,727	2,790	2,834	2,868	2,861	2,848	2,831	2,798	2,735
Speech or language impairments	1,302	1,168	985	1,015	1,022	1,045	1,060	1,068	1,080	1,409	1,391	1,412	1,441	1,463	1,468
Mental retardation	961	830	534	555	571	579	589	597	600	624	616	602	593	578	556
Emotional disturbance	283	347	389	427	437	446	454	462	469	481	483	485	489	489	477
Hearing impairments	88	79	58	64	67	68	69	70	71	78	78	78	79	79	79
Orthopedic impairments	87	58	49	60	63	66	67	69	71	83	83	83	77	73	71
Other health impairments[a]	141	98	55	106	133	160	190	220	253	303	350	403	464	521	570
Visual impairments	38	31	23	24	25	25	26	26	26	29	28	29	28	29	29
Multiple disabilities	—	68	96	88	93	98	106	106	111	133	136	138	140	140	141
Deaf-blindness	—	3	1	1	1	1	1	2	2	1	2	2	2	2	2
Autism	—	—	—	22	28	34	42	53	65	94	114	137	163	191	223
Traumatic brain injury	—	—	—	7	9	10	12	13	14	16	22	22	23	24	24
Developmental delay	—	—	—	—	—	—	2	12	19	178	242	283	305	332	339
Preschool disabled[b]	†	†	390	519	544	555	565	568	581	†	†	†	†	†	†
Percentage distribution of children served															
All disabilities	100.0	100.0	100.0	100.0	100.0	100.0	100.0	100.0	100.0	100.0	100.0	100.0	100.0	100.0	100.0
Specific learning disabilities	21.5	35.3	45.2	46.3	46.3	46.2	46.2	46.1	45.7	45.5	44.7	43.7	42.7	41.6	40.7
Speech or language impairments	35.2	28.2	20.9	18.9	18.3	18.2	17.9	17.6	17.4	22.4	21.7	21.6	21.7	21.8	21.9
Mental retardation	26.0	20.0	11.3	10.3	10.2	10.1	10.0	9.9	9.7	9.9	9.6	9.2	8.9	8.6	8.3
Emotional disturbance	7.7	8.4	8.3	7.9	7.8	7.8	7.7	7.6	7.6	7.6	7.5	7.4	7.4	7.3	7.1

(continues)

Table 2.1 (*continued*)

Type of disability	1976-77	1980-81	1990-91	1994-95	1995-96	1996-97	1997-98	1998-99	1999-2000	2000-01	2001-02	2002-03	2003-04	2004-05	2005-06
1	2	3	4	5	6	7	8	9	10	11	12	13	14	15	16
Percentage distribution of children served															
Hearing impairments	2.4	1.9	1.2	1.2	1.2	1.2	1.2	1.2	1.1	1.2	1.2	1.2	1.2	1.2	1.2
Orthopedic impairments	2.4	1.4	1.0	1.1	1.1	1.1	1.1	1.1	1.1	1.3	1.3	1.3	1.2	1.1	1.1
Other health impairments[a]	3.8	2.4	1.2	2.0	2.4	2.8	3.2	3.6	4.1	4.8	5.5	6.2	7.0	7.7	8.5
Visual impairments	1.0	0.7	0.5	0.4	0.4	0.4	0.4	0.4	0.4	0.5	0.4	0.4	0.4	0.4	0.4
Multiple disabilities	—	1.6	2.0	1.6	1.7	1.7	1.8	1.8	1.8	2.1	2.1	2.1	2.1	2.1	2.1
Deaf-blindness	—	0.1	#	#	#	#	#	#	#	#	#	#	#	#	#
Autism	—	—	—	0.4	0.5	0.6	0.7	0.9	1.0	1.5	1.8	2.1	2.5	2.8	3.3
Traumatic brain injury	—	—	—	0.1	0.2	0.2	0.2	0.2	0.2	0.2	0.3	0.3	0.4	0.4	0.4
Developmental delay	—	—	—	—	—	—	0.0	0.2	0.3	2.8	3.8	4.3	4.6	4.9	5.1
Preschool disabled[b]	†	†	8.3	9.7	9.8	9.7	9.6	9.4	9.4	†	†	†	†	†	†
Number served as a percent of total enrollment[c]															
All disabilities	8.3	10.1	11.4	12.2	12.4	12.6	12.8	13.0	13.2	13.3	13.4	13.5	13.7	13.8	13.8
Specific learning disabilities	1.8	3.6	5.2	5.6	5.8	5.8	5.9	6.0	6.0	6.1	6.0	5.9	5.8	5.7	5.6
Speech or language impairments	2.9	2.9	2.4	2.3	2.3	2.3	2.3	2.3	2.3	3.0	2.9	2.9	3.0	3.0	3.0
Mental retardation	2.2	2.0	1.3	1.3	1.3	1.3	1.3	1.3	1.3	1.3	1.3	1.2	1.2	1.2	1.1
Emotional disturbance	0.6	0.8	0.9	1.0	1.0	1.0	1.0	1.0	1.0	1.0	1.0	1.0	1.0	1.0	1.0
Hearing impairments	0.2	0.2	0.1	0.1	0.1	0.1	0.1	0.2	0.2	0.2	0.2	0.2	0.2	0.2	0.2
Orthopedic impairments	0.2	0.1	0.1	0.1	0.1	0.1	0.1	0.1	0.2	0.2	0.2	0.2	0.2	0.2	0.1
Other health impairments[a]	0.3	0.2	0.1	0.2	0.3	0.4	0.4	0.5	0.5	0.6	0.7	0.8	1.0	1.1	1.2
Visual impairments	0.1	0.1	0.1	0.1	0.1	0.1	0.1	0.1	0.1	0.1	0.1	0.1	0.1	0.1	0.1
Multiple disabilities	—	0.2	0.2	0.2	0.2	0.2	0.2	0.2	0.3	0.3	0.3	0.3	0.3	0.3	0.3
Deaf-blindness	—	#	#	#	#	#	#	#	#	#	#	#	#	#	#
Autism	—	—	—	#	0.1	0.1	0.1	0.1	0.1	0.2	0.2	0.3	0.3	0.4	0.5

(*continues*)

Table 2.1 (*continued*)

Type of disability	1976-77	1980-81	1990-91	1994-95	1995-96	1996-97	1997-98	1998-99	1999-2000	2000-01	2001-02	2002-03	2003-04	2004-05	2005-06
1	2	3	4	5	6	7	8	9	10	11	12	13	14	15	16
						Number served as a percent of total enrollment[c]									
Traumatic brain injury	—	—	—	#	#	#	#	#	#	#	#	#	#	#	0.1
Developmental delay	—	—	—	—	—	—	#	#	#	0.4	0.5	0.6	0.6	0.7	0.7
Preschool disabled[a]	†	†	0.9	1.2	1.2	1.2	1.2	1.2	1.2	†	†	†	†	†	†

Note. Includes students served under Chapter 1 of the Elementary and Secondary Education Act and under the Individuals With Disabilities Education Act (IDEA), formerly the Education of the Handicapped Act. Prior to October 1994, children and youth with disabilities were served under Chapter 1 as well as IDEA, Part B. In October 1994, funding for children and youth with disabilities was consolidated under IDEA, Part B. Data reported in this table for years prior to 1994–95 include children ages 0–21 served under Chapter 1. Counts are based on reports from the 50 states and the District of Columbia only (i.e., table excludes data for other jurisdictions). Increases since 1987–88 are due in part to legislation enacted in fall 1986, which added a mandate for public school special education services for 3– to 5-year-old children with disabilities. Some data have been revised from previously published figures. Detail may not sum to totals because of rounding.

—Not available.

† Not applicable.

Rounds to zero.

[a] Other health impairments include having limited strength, vitality, or alertness due to chronic or acute health problems such as a heart condition, tuberculosis, rheumatic fever, nephritis, asthma, sickle cell anemia, hemophilia, epilepsy, lead poisoning, leukemia, or diabetes.

[b] Includes preschool children ages 3–5 served under Chapter 1 and IDEA, Part B. Prior to 1987–88, these students were included in the counts by disability condition. Beginning in 1987–88, states were no longer required to report preschool children (ages 0–5) by disability condition. Beginning in 2000–01, preschool children were again identified by disability condition.

[c] Based on the total enrollment in public schools, prekindergarten through 12th grade.

Source: U.S. Department of Education, Office of Special Education and Rehabilitative Services, *Annual Report to Congress on the Implementation of the Individuals With Disabilities Education Act*, selected years, 1977 through 2005; and Individuals With Disabilities Education Act (IDEA) database, retrieved on September 22, 2006, from http://www.ideadata.org/PartBdata.asp; National Center for Education Statistics, *Statistics of Public Elementary and Secondary School Systems*, 1977; Common Core of Data (CCD), "State Nonfiscal Survey of Public Elementary/Secondary Education," 1981–82 through 2004–05; and *Projections of Education Statistics to 2015*. (This table was prepared September 2006.) Reprinted from Institute of Educational Sciences, Department of Education Web site. Available online (http://nces.ed.gov/programs/digest/d06/tables/dt06_048.asp).

be careful to avoid any generalizations about the personality style of any special education student.

Like mainstream students, students with disabilities display the full range of personality patterns, from normal, healthy personalities to troubled personalities that exhibit defiance, immaturity, dependency, anxiety, depression, or passive aggression. Our focus in this section is restricted to students with disabilities who are passive aggressive. Furthermore, we are excluding those students with a disability who were classified as socialized by Pathways 1, 2, and 3, described previously in this chapter. These students would have developed a passive-aggressive personality independently of their disability. Our Pathway 4 personality is restricted to those students with disabilities for whom the disability and failed expectations are the contributing factors in the development of a passive-aggressive personality.

The Impact of a Disability on Personality Development

Students with disabilities are first and foremost children moving through the normal stages of life. Disabilities, however, prevent some children from attaining the goals of each developmental stage within the expected time frame. This is especially true for children with learning disabilities and emotional disorders whose disabilities are not readily apparent to others. Because of the "invisibility" of some disabilities and disorders, parents and teachers may enforce a set of expectations that are unachievable for these children. Over time, the persistent inability to meet expectations causes a child to feel different from others. They often are seen as being difficult by their parents, teachers, and peers.

When children have difficulty achieving their developmental goals or meeting the expectations of others, they not only become frustrated by their lack of performance, but also begin to feel inadequate. This sense of inadequacy is not a one-time occurrence but rather an ongoing problem that impacts their fragile self-esteem. We believe that the fourth pathway to passive-aggressive personality development is paved by this dynamic; the child with a disability who has failed in the eyes of his or her parents and significant adults may cope with feelings of inadequacy by developing a passive-aggressive personality.

Unfortunately, the adolescent years only exacerbate this troubling developmental situation. The demands and pressures to catch up academically, to prepare for a vocation, to be accepted by their peers, and to become independent only fuel the child's feelings of incompetence and inadequacy. Children coping with disabilities and failed expectations may have marginal frustration tolerance around specific tasks, misperceive social interactions with others, have limited attention spans, and have low self-esteem. Their social–emotional needs dominate their behavior and disrupt academic progress and interpersonal relationships. Passive-aggressive behaviors, through which adolescents with disabilities can act out their anger in socially acceptable, barely perceptible (at the moment) ways, become entrenched ways of relating.

What Children With Disabilities Hear From Some Parents

First, we offer a word of support for parents of children with disabilities. These parents deserve all the support, encouragement, and skill that professionals can provide them. Maintaining a family in the 21st century is not an easy accomplishment under the best of circumstances. The pressures to find rewarding work and economic security, to maintain positive familial relations, to care for extended relatives, and to plan for the future are all time-consuming and stressful. On top of these daily stressors, what happens when a parent discovers that his or her child has a disability?

Larry Silver (1992), a child psychiatrist, described the normal reactions many parents have in this situation. He believes that parents of children with learning disabilities go through the following three emotional stages (pp. 92–96):

- Denial: "There must be a mistake. It can't be true."

- Anger: "Why us? This is not fair."

- Guilt: "It must be my fault."

He also found that parents who received and were receptive to psychological counseling were able to work through these stages and end up becoming realistic advocates for their child. This would be ideal for all families, but some parents seem to be stuck in the stages of anger and guilt. Over time, the stress and responsibility of meeting the expanding needs of their child wears them down. They feel overwhelmed and defeated. During these emotional times, the parents give in to their feelings of helplessness, and their child may hear the following impulsive and depreciating comments:

- "We never should have had children."

- "Why are we being punished?"

- "After all we have done for you, I don't understand why you aren't more appreciative."

- "You are not using your brain or meeting your potential."

- "You are lazy and undisciplined and only think of your own needs."

- "You think you know everything, so you never listen to people who want to help you."

- "If you had a better attitude, your life would be better."

- "I'm sick and tired of trying to help you. You are impossible."

- "You put off everything until the last minute, so you will fail."

What Children With Disabilities Hear From Some Teachers

The demands on teachers and school personnel are likewise overwhelming. The primary objective of attending to the individual needs of a child with disabilities gets easily shoved aside by the multiple priorities and demands of general classroom management, federal mandates, and test scores. Teachers often learn the hard way that troubled children know how to short-circuit traditional attempts at classroom control. When feeling frustrated and powerless, teachers may give students impulsive and depreciating feedback:

- "You are smart, but you are not motivated to learn."
- "You are more interested in fooling around and acting silly with your friends than you are in doing your assignment."
- "You could learn if you paid attention to my instructions."
- "You overreact to any corrections I make."
- "You enjoy messing up."
- "You are afraid to try anything new."
- "You spend too much time doing insignificant things instead of doing the important ones."
- "You always have an excuse for everything."

What Children With Disabilities Hear From Some Peers

Peers often fail to be sensitive and compassionate to others, particularly to students who appear different. Some special education students have been teased, humiliated, and scapegoated by their peers, resulting in feelings of rejection and anger. Here is a sampling of some of the names and comments that special education students have heard:

- *Retardo*
- *Weirdo*
- *Geek*
- "You don't get it, so get lost."
- "Nobody likes you."
- "Did you ride in on the short bus this morning?"
- "What's the matter—forget to take your meds this morning?"

What Children With Disabilities Say to Themselves

Children become what they hear others say about them. Over time, they internalize negative messages and come to believe that they are innately damaged, deficient, and dysfunctional. When angry, they resent and passively oppose any attempt to behave at the level expected by others. Messages like the ones in the following list become part of the child's belief system and guide the child as self-fulfilling prophecy:

- "I am a disappointment to others."
- "No matter how hard I try, I can't meet the expectations of my mom, dad, teachers, and friends."
- "Nothing has ever worked out for me. Nothing ever will."
- "No one appreciates me."
- "No one understands how hard I try and how much I struggle."
- "If I try this and fail, everyone will make fun of me."

- "I can't stand to be made a fool of again!"
- "Life is so unfair!"

Our years of work, combined with the cumulative observations of professionals, parents, and adults with passive-aggressive personalities, compel us to believe that some children with disabilities protect themselves from feelings of inadequacy and rejection by becoming passive aggressive. Through passive-aggressive means, kids who too often feel powerless gain a sense of control by getting others to act out the covert anger they harbor deep within. Children whose very intelligence may be doubted due to their disability can be quite clever in their opposition to authority, "misbehaving" through hostile cooperation and compliant defiance.

Summary of the Four Developmental Pathways to Passive-Aggressive Personalities

In this chapter, we have explored the four developmental pathways that most commonly lay the foundation of the passive-aggressive personality:

- The socializing force underlying a Pathway 1 passive-aggressive personality is early, prolonged, and excessive psychological and physical abuse resulting in the expression of hidden anger based on fear.

- The socializing force underlying a Pathway 2 passive-aggressive personality is early, prolonged, and excessive socialization around values of goodness, social acceptance, and guilt that encourage a child to suppress anger by expressing it indirectly.

- The socializing force underlying a Pathway 3 passive-aggressive personality is the dysfunctional dynamic of the triangular family. It is based on the son or daughter who carries the passive-aggressive message to the targeted dominant parent with such determination that the child is willing to sabotage his or her own life to succeed.

- The socializing force underlying a Pathway 4 passive-aggressive personality is a child with a disability who has failed in the eyes of his or her parents and significant adults and copes with feelings of inadequacy by developing a passive-aggressive personality.

> The child with a disability who has failed in the eyes of her parents may cope with feelings of inadequacy by developing a passive-aggressive personality.

These socializing forces instill in developing children a set of passive-aggressive thoughts, feelings, and behaviors that guide them in their interactions with most people, across nearly all situations.

In Chapter 3, we continue along these pathways, examining the four key psychological reasons that individuals behave passive aggressively in school, at home, in close adult relationships, and in the workplace. We will compare isolated, situational, and group-specific passive-aggressive behaviors with passive aggression as a way of life—the personality style demonstrated by children socialized along a passive-aggressive pathway.

3

Reasons People Use Passive-Aggressive Behaviors

William rushes to social studies class so that he can sit next to Ellie. He has had a crush on her all year, but seems to always miss out on opportunities to talk to her. When Mr. Conway instructs him to return to his regular seat in the back of the room, William is humiliated and angry. He moves his seat without verbal protest, but spends the rest of the class period sharpening his pencil, asking to use the bathroom, having uncontrollable coughing fits, and waving his hand in the air to comment on every point made by Mr. Conway.

As we learned in Chapter 2, there are distinctive pathways to the development of the passive-aggressive personality. Passive-aggressive behavior also exists in varying degrees, ranging from normal to pathological, and can differ in its impact. William's adolescent antics, inspired by his crush on Ellie, are disruptive to the social studies lesson, and undoubtedly irritating to Mr. Conway that day, but they represent a single incident of annoying defiance, easily traced to a cause. More damaging passive-aggressive behaviors are those that exist as part of a consistent personal pattern, spread across most situations, that leave a trail of academic impairment, relationship damage, and workplace disruption in their wake. From our study and experiences, we have identified four reasons why individuals behave passive aggressively:

1. situational response to adult demands

2. developmental stage

3. characteristic of a cultural norm or ethnic group

4. a way of life

As we explore these four reasons, we will make a critical distinction between the first three, which represent passive-aggressive behaviors chosen by individuals to achieve specific ends, and the final reason, which is indicative of a pathological and pervasive passive-aggressive personality style.

Passive-Aggressive Behavior as a Situational Response to Adult Demands

All of us have been in situations in which a parent, teacher, spouse, or boss makes a demand or sets an expectation that we are unwilling or unable to fulfill at the time.

A. "I want this room cleaned up now!"

B. "If your assignment is not in by the end of this class, you will get a zero!"

C. "Would you mind hanging the shelf in the upstairs hallway today?"

D. "Have that sales report on my desk by 9 A.M. tomorrow."

Instead of expressing our anger openly, we may choose to respond to these demands and expectations in a passive-aggressive manner. For example, we may feign confusion:

A. "What do you mean, Mom? It's not even dirty. I'm using all of those pieces to build my fort!"

Or we may pretend not to see, hear, or remember the assignment:

B. "Oh, I totally forgot about it! I was so busy tutoring Kevin with his science that I forgot all about my own math homework. Can I get it to you tomorrow?"

Or we may procrastinate:

C. "I was planning on hanging it right after dinner, but I didn't have the bracket I needed. I ran to the hardware store to get it, but now the kids are asleep. Are you sure you want me hammering the wall?"

Or we may behave in ways that will delay and frustrate the standards of the evaluating authority:

D. "I'll have that report to you first thing tomorrow, sir," says Leanna. The next morning, she calls in sick with a "sudden flu."

In these examples, as well as in the one that is to follow, the person's intent is not to argue with or confront the authority. The goal is to behave in a socially acceptable way while defying or getting back at the authority figure.

> **The goal is to behave in a socially acceptable way while defying or getting back at the authority figure.**

Richard liked to relax at night when he got home from work. He loved his family, but when it came to the evening hours, he wanted time to himself. And for the month of January, he had had it this way. In helping their 2-year-old daughter, Hayley, adjust to a "big-girl bed," his wife Kelly had taken full responsibility for the bedtime routine. By February, Hayley was able to settle down within 15 minutes and stay in her bed to fall asleep. One night, Kelly asked Richard if he could put Hayley to bed. Richard agreed with the request and went upstairs with Hayley.

From downstairs, Kelly could hear squeals of laughter. She thought to herself, "How nice that they are getting some playtime together!" After 20 minutes passed by, she heard the loud slam of a closet door, and wondered if Hayley needed a new diaper or change of pajamas. When 30 minutes had gone by and loud music started to play from Hayley's room, Kelly could feel her anger rising. Forty-five minutes after she asked Richard and Hayley to go upstairs for bedtime, Kelly went up to the room and opened the door. Hayley was out of her fleece pajamas and into a bathing suit, sun hat, Dora the Explorer sunglasses, and a pair of brand new, too-big, hot pink water shoes.

Hayley ran to her mother with a huge, wide-awake smile! "Bedtime so fun!"

Kelly glared at Richard and exited the room quickly. When he returned downstairs another 35 minutes later and faced Kelly's angry barrage of questions about what he was thinking and why he would defy the soothing bedtime routine she had worked so hard to create, Richard simply said, "What? We were just having some fun!"

The situation was clear; Richard didn't want to be bothered with bedtime routines. Rather than tell Kelly this fact and risk an argument over sharing child-care responsibilities, he chose a passive-aggressive response to the situation. The cunning of his personal choice was unmistakable: If Kelly had argued with his stated intention of having fun with his daughter, she would surely have appeared as an uptight, no-fun mother and overly controlling wife. Richard's strategy in the situation was a winning one for both him and Hayley. Hayley thoroughly enjoyed bedtime that night and thought her Daddy was the coolest in the world, and Richard was not called upon to help with this evening responsibility for months to come.

While these responses are clear examples of passive-aggressive behaviors, they do not represent an individual's only way, or even his or her typical way, of responding to frustrating requests and situations. In other situations, these people may choose to behave in a manner that is assertive, humorous, aggressive, regressed, dependent, or diplomatic. Healthy individuals know a variety of ways of responding to difficult situations and expressing anger. For them, passive-aggressive behavior is a *personal choice* and not a habitual or predictable response to an authority figure. This kind of passive-aggressive behavior is a function of the situation rather than an ingrained personality trait.

Passive-Aggressive Behavior as a Developmental Stage

Most kids go through predictable stages of passive-aggressive behavior at home by targeting their parents. What some parents describe as the stubborn, irresponsible, lazy, forgetful, or irritating behavior of their adolescent (or even their preschooler) may be nothing more than a thinly disguised layer of passive-aggressive behavior.

Developmentally, a typical 16-year-old boy has achieved close to 100% of his height, intellectual potential, and sexuality but only about 20% of his economic and personal freedom. Conflict occurs when the adolescent's desire to be independent of adult control and supervision runs counter to the realities of his place in life. The adolescent still is dependent on his parents for most basic living needs such as room, food, clothing, transportation, education, and money.

Intertwined with these dependencies are almost endless sources of potential conflict between a typical adolescent and his or her parents. They may differ on issues such as the following:

- appearance

- manners and language

- study habits and grades

- chores

- music

- friends

- dating rules and curfew

- use of drugs and alcohol

- use of the family car

- academic and vocational goals

- moral and ethical standards

Whether they enjoy it or not, responsible parents often must interfere with their adolescent's immediate plans and pleasures by setting limits on behavior and providing natural consequences for acts of irresponsibility. Given these developmental conditions, parent–adolescent conflict can be seen as a very normal, even healthy, reaction to the push-pull of ever-increasing adolescent independence, moderated by protective adult limit-setting. As parents set standards and impose limits, they wield the manifest power in the familial relationship. The adolescent is often cast into a role of being subservient and compliant.

While many of the common issues may be negotiated with little or no conflict, when the right issues do bring conflict, an adolescent's typical response is to become either openly rebellious or passive aggressive. Most adolescents, after testing the rebellion option, end up choosing to become passive aggressive at home: They find passive-aggressive behavior to be a more satisfying way of frustrating their parents. Their repertoire may include endless ways of procrastinating, forgetting, not hearing, and completing their chores at an unacceptable level of performance that drive their parents crazy, such as in this example, shared by one of our seminar participants:

> I asked my 15-year-old daughter to load the dishwasher. After I'd asked her to do it several times, my voice growing louder and louder, she slowly moved to the dishwasher and began to load our dinner dishes—without removing the leftover food. I reminded her to scrape the food off first. She said, "Okay," but continued to not scrape the dishes.
>
> After several reminders, I couldn't stand it anymore. I angrily said, "Never mind! I will do it myself!" She put down the dish and calmly replied, "Don't ever say I won't load the dishwasher."

It should be noted that younger children are perfectly capable of exhibiting a similar (albeit less sophisticated) array of passive-aggressive behaviors. Like their adolescent counterparts, who learn that passive aggression is more satisfying (and usually less likely to result in punishment) than overt aggression, children moving from toddlerhood into the preschool years catch on to the fact that tantrums in the candy aisle will result in being whisked out of a store, but pretending not to hear mommy say "Look but don't touch" can easily result in an "accidentally" unwrapped candy bar and subsequent chocolate purchase!

Fortunately, the incidents of preschool and adolescent passive aggression described here are representative of temporary and normative developmental behaviors that usually exist only within close familial relationships and not in other areas of the child's life. In Chapter 5 we will present more examples of young people using passive-aggressive behavior to get back at their parents and siblings at home.

Passive-Aggressive Behavior as a Characteristic of a Cultural Norm or Ethnic Group

Some cultures and ethnic groups set absolute standards for the need to be polite and charming, regardless of internal feelings. In the example of Eve, in Chapter 2, we described how early, prolonged, and excessive socialization along standards of goodness, social approval, and guilt can lead to the development of a passive-aggressive personality. She is the classic example of southern hospitality, immortalized in literature and film, being cordial and congenial in all social situations, and inhibiting and controlling negative and confrontational interactions, even when they are merited.

Certain cultures expect children to show respect for their elders and authority figures. For example, many Asian families teach their children to honor the status of their elders and to be submissive and obedient to their wishes and demands. Even if children are upset by the judgments or decisions their elders make, they are taught to swallow their anger and never to debate, argue, or confront their elders. Any overt expression of anger toward one's elders is labeled undesirable and results in *losing face* in the family and community. The suppression of aggression toward elders may create a level of civility and politeness that is admirable, but it also creates for some children and youth a reservoir of unexpressed hostile thoughts, a long memory of personal depreciation, and the development of passive-aggressive behavior toward select people at select times.

> Julia was the third child born to Japanese-immigrant parents. Both of her parents were medical doctors, and her two older siblings were both enrolled in pre-med courses at Ivy League universities. Julia's parents expected her to follow the same pathway. Although just as intelligent as her family members, Julia preferred the performing arts to the sciences and wanted to attend art school rather than a traditional 4-year college. During her senior year in high school, Julia followed her parents' wishes and submitted applications to 11 top-ranked universities, including both of her siblings' schools. What none of her family members knew, however, is that in each of her essays, Julia asked admissions committee members not to accept her application to their school. When she received "rejection" letters from every 4-year university to which she had applied, her parents suggested to her that perhaps she should consider applying to Juilliard.

A third example of this reason for using passive-aggressive behavior involves members of various customer-service industries. Many service professionals, including restaurant workers and salespersons, are expected to demonstrate hospitable behaviors. When faced with demanding patrons, customers, and citizens, however, these individuals may demonstrate passive-aggressive behaviors, as in the following case:

Sharon went to the customer-service counter of a local supercenter to return a pair of brand-new, never-worn shoes she had purchased on clearance the previous day. The tags were still on the shoes and Sharon had her receipt in hand. After waiting in line for what she felt was an unreasonable length of time, Sharon's exasperation was apparent to the customer-service representative. "I'm in a hurry!" she barked when it was her turn in line. "I want a refund on these shoes."

The young woman behind the counter smiled graciously and took the shoes from Sharon. She began to inspect them.

"There's nothing wrong with them!" said Sharon.

"No problem, Ma'am," said the worker. "I just have to check. Do you have your receipt?"

Sharon threw the receipt at her. "I just bought them yesterday. I never wore them. They are the wrong color. And they look so cheap. Everything in this store is hideous."

The worker, continuing to smile, looked at the receipt carefully and replied, "I'm sorry, Ma'am, but these shoes were purchased on clearance. We have a no-return policy on clearance items. All sales are final."

"I want to speak to your manager!" yelled Sharon. "This is ridiculous! How dare you?"

"Certainly, Ma'am. All referrals to management are handled at that counter," she said, pointing to a line, 10 people deep, across the aisle.

Fuming, Sharon grabbed her shoes and walked out of the store.

The next customer in line overheard the loud scene created by Sharon. As soon as she approached the counter, she politely explained that she too had a clearance item for return and would move on to the other line. The customer-service representative stopped her, saying, "No problem. I'd be happy to take care of that for you right here."

In the cultural, ethnic, and group-specific dynamics represented here, passive aggression is used as a behavior of choice within a particular situation. Eve, Julia, and the customer-service representative all make choices to behave in a passive-aggressive manner to achieve specific, desired outcomes. This is an important distinction: The conscious decision to behave in a passive-aggressive manner in a particular situation or within a certain group setting is different from passive aggression as a way of life.

Passive-Aggressive Personality as a Way of Life

For Richard, who does not want to be involved in the bedtime routine; for a 15-year-old who would rather chat on MySpace than load the dishwasher, and for Julia, who is desperate to enroll in art school, passive-aggressive behaviors are occasional, calculated means to specific, desired ends. They represent a surface level of emotional and behavioral dishonesty, but they are not rooted in suppressed anger or hostile revenge. Passive aggression is distinguished as a pathological and problematic way of life only when it goes beyond a situational response, a developmental stage, or a culture-bound behavior and becomes pervasive across most situations.

As noted in Chapter 2, the development of a passive-aggressive personality is a complex psychological process. It begins with the early, prolonged, and excessive socialization of angry feelings and behavior in children. Over time, a child internalizes a characteristic way of perceiving, thinking, feeling, and behaving during times of anger, which ultimately results in the development of a passive-aggressive personality. This unique way a child organizes the world becomes his or her psychological character and personal style of relating during most stressful situations. A passive-aggressive adult often recreates the dynamics of childhood—even when the situation does not call for or warrant it.

> Passive aggression is identified as a pathological and problematic way of life only when it goes beyond a situational response, a developmental stage, or a culture-bound behavior and becomes pervasive across most social situations.

When we began to study passive aggression, we believed that most passive-aggressive behaviors were driven by hidden and unconscious feelings of anger and hatred. We hypothesized that passive-aggressive individuals relied mostly upon unconscious defense mechanisms, such as denial, rationalization, projection, and displacement. After talking with hundreds of passive-aggressive children and adults over the years, however, we have changed our view. We are now convinced that the majority of passive-aggressive behaviors are consciously motivated.

We find, for example, that when students are confronted about their passive-aggressive behavior, they usually respond by saying, "I don't know what you're talking about." But if we simultaneously observe their nonverbal behavior when we confront them, a different message usually emerges; they often give a half-smile, shift their eyes, or cock their heads in a revealing way. This lets us know that our comment about their behavior is accurate. A few passive-aggressive persons, much to our surprise, have told us privately and with delightful satisfaction how enjoyable, rewarding, and effective it is to be passive aggressive. It appears that a few passive-aggressive people receive an abundant amount of self-reinforcing pleasure from their characteristic behavior.

> Benign Confrontation is a verbal intervention skill in which the adult gently but openly shares his thoughts about the person's behavior and unexpressed anger. It is based on the decision not to silently accept the person's manipulative and controlling behavior any longer.

In the chapters that follow, you will learn to distinguish between various levels of passive-aggressive behavior and understand how this behavior pervades schools, homes, and workplaces. The

Passive-Aggressive Conflict Cycle will be used to explain the complex dynamics of hidden and masked anger and show you how to effectively interrupt this troublesome cycle, bringing anger into the open, where it can be met head on. You will gain important verbal strategies for effectively dealing with passive-aggressive behavior. The skill of Benign Confrontation will guide you in establishing more honest and more productive relationships with the passive-aggressive person who keeps flashing you his angry smile.

The Five Levels of Passive-Aggressive Behavior

4

Passive-aggressive individuals use a diverse and sophisticated arsenal of guerilla warfare tactics to express anger and hostility toward others in covert but often successful ways. What they say and do is masked behind compliance and civility, making their anger hard to detect and frustrating to experience. This chapter is based on the analysis of several thousand written examples of real-life passive-aggressive behavior. Through our study, we identified five distinct levels of passive aggression. A working knowledge of these levels is useful in understanding

- the varied ways that passive aggression is manifested in behavior and

- the range of passive aggression that exists, from common, everyday behaviors to pathological acts of aggression.

This chapter defines and distinguishes each of the five levels, from the most common to the most destructive (see Figure 4.1). You will gain skills for recognizing passive aggression in its diverse forms and understand where frustrating behaviors in school, home, and the workplace fall within these levels.

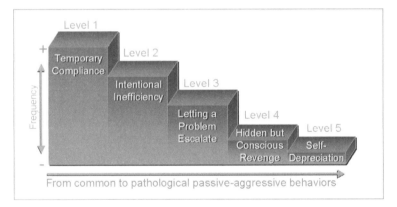

Figure 4.1. The five levels of passive-aggressive behavior. *Note*. From *The Angry Smile: Understanding and Managing Passive Aggressive Behavior of Students and Staff*, by N. J. Long, October 1998, paper presented at the Conflict Cycle Paradigm, KidsPeace National Center for Kids in Crisis, 16th National Conference, Allendale, PA. Copyright 1998 by KidsPeace. Reprinted with permission.

Level 1: Temporary Compliance
"I'm coming!"

At Level 1 (temporary compliance), the passive-aggressive individual verbally agrees to comply with a request but behaviorally delays or consciously forgets to carry it out. This is the most common form of passive-aggressive behavior and is readily observed in school, at home, in close adult relationships, and in the workplace.

> Level 1: The person verbally agrees but behaviorally delays.

The essential feature of this most widely used passive-aggressive tactic is that the individual does not argue or resist the request that is made of him or her. Unlike an oppositional student in a classroom, whose loud protests invite obvious repercussions from a teacher, the passive-aggressive person's defiance is audibly undetectable. The subtlety of the tactic is precisely what leaves the teacher so flustered and confused over what to do; teachers have a strong set of classroom guidelines for managing openly disruptive behavior but less instruction on how to handle covert defiance. Their lack of insight on how to best manage passive-aggressive behavior is exactly what makes the behavior thrive! Whereas the openly oppositional student loses with an immediate deduction of privileges or trip to a crisis room, the passive-aggressive student wins immediate gratification by witnessing his or her teacher's frustration and often never having to comply with the original request.

Following are several examples of Level 1 passive aggression:

- The child is involved in watching her favorite movie and does not want to turn it off. When her mother asks her to set the table for dinner, she shouts, "OK, Mom!" but never moves a muscle.

- A student is convinced that compliance with her teacher's request to read aloud will expose her learning disability, so she forgets to bring her book to group.

- A husband is upset with his wife over an issue from the previous day. Rather than get entangled in a heated discussion, he graciously takes her "supplies" list on his run to the hardware store but claims to have lost it when he returns home without her items.

- An employee believes her supervisor's request is beneath her abilities, so she nods her approval at the assignment and then places it at the bottom of her in-box.

In each of these examples, it is the underlying feeling of anger toward the requesting person that defines the behavior as passive aggressive.

Passive aggression at this level is the most common, everyday form of the behavior. For this reason, it is also the kind that most often goes by unnoticed. With each act of passive aggression, the child/student/husband/employee discharges a small piece of his or her anger—like a drip of water. With every act of ignoring it, the mother/teacher/wife/boss catches the drip in his or her reservoir of anger. The classic scenario is the receiver not acknowledging the small, irritating acts of aggression, because to do so would seem petty; but when their holding tank inevitably overflows, they unleash floodwaters of accumulated anger. The passive-aggressive person, dry as a bone, watches it all happen with satisfaction.

In Chapter 10, "The Passive-Aggressive Conflict Cycle," we examine in detail just how these minor irritations add up to major explosions. The lesson to take from temporary compliance is that a red flag should be raised whenever a person's words do not match his or her behaviors. While not all such incidents will be representative of passive-aggressive behavior, many of them will be, and the ability to recognize passive aggression—even at its lower levels—will go a long way in preventing emotional flooding.

Level 2: Intentional Inefficiency
"I'll do it my way"

Level 2 (intentional inefficiency) is a more sophisticated form of passive-aggressive behavior. The individual at this level complies with a given request but carries it out in an unacceptable way. Some examples:

> **Level 2: The person complies with a request but carries it out in an unacceptable manner.**

- As assigned, a teenage son vacuums the entire house after school. When his parents arrive home, they find every piece of furniture moved from its place and small dents in the wooden furniture from where the vacuum cleaner hit them.

- A student hands in homework that is messy.

- A husband prepares a well-done steak for his wife, though he knows she prefers to eat them rare.

- An employee dramatically overspends his budget on an important project.

At Level 2, the individual is upset over the request but feels pressure from the authority figure to immediately carry out the particular chore, task, or assignment. The passive-aggressive person knows from experience that to engage in Level 1 delaying tactics or to debate the request would be useless in the situation. As noted in our first example, that of Jason, the passive-aggressive person is usually quite bright and astute at understanding his target's emotional buttons. He knows what will and won't work across varied situations and selects the "right" level of passive-aggressive behavior—that which will bring him satisfaction and keep his underlying anger under wraps.

In Level 2, the passive-aggressive person's solution is to complete the task but to do it in a way that will not meet the minimum standards of the evaluator. As a result, the parent, teacher, spouse, or coworker becomes so upset by the level of performance that he or she usually ends up doing the task. A typical Level 2 statement might be "I don't know why she's so upset; I did what she asked me to do! Her trouble is she wants everything done her way—perfectly."

In the end, the passive-aggressive person has been successful on three counts:

1. justifying his or her behavior,

2. making the requestor angry, and

3. probably not being asked to complete the same (or similar) task in the future.

Given these seemingly positive objectives, it is important to recall that the passive-aggressive person wins by losing. While she gains temporary emotional satisfaction by getting the other person to act out his or her anger, in the long term, she damages important relationships all across her life and frustrates those who could otherwise be her best allies. The passive-aggressive person's lack of authentic relationships and inability to express emotions honestly and directly means that in the end, all of his or her wins add up to a substantial loss.

Level 3: Letting a Problem Escalate "Oops! I'm sorry it happened"

Level 3 (letting a problem escalate) is a more deliberate and serious way of expressing personal anger toward another person by choosing not to share some knowledge when it would prevent a problem. The Level 3 passive-aggressive person realizes that by not acting on her knowledge or observation, her teacher or parent, spouse or colleague, will have an immediate problem.

> Level 3: The person uses inaction to allow a foreseeable problem to escalate and takes pleasure in the resulting anguish.

While getting ready for school in the morning, Chris hears a news story on the radio of a major accident on the interstate that has resulted in a 6-mile traffic stoppage. Although he knows this is the route his father will be traveling to the airport, he is still upset over their argument from the previous night, so he decides not to pass on the news.

By doing nothing, Chris allows the problem to happen. He enjoys the thought of his father's anguish as he inevitably sits in traffic and worries about making his flight on time.

Level 3 passive-aggressive strategies are guilt-free expressions of hostility. The passive-aggressive person can honestly say that he or she didn't *do* anything to create the problem. These are crimes of omission:

A. Ava is aware that the car needs gas as her mother leaves the house for a meeting, but she doesn't say anything.

B. Laurel knows that her sister's dog has been cooped up in the house all day, but she doesn't let the dog out.

C. Tom receives an important phone call for his wife but says nothing about it.

Ava, Laurel, and Tom are adept at justifying their lack of action by voicing several rationalizations (accompanied by a smile):

A. "I'm sorry, but I thought you realized the tank was near empty. You knew that I used the car to drive all the way across town yesterday."

B. "It's not my job to take care of your pet. I thought Dad would let her out. Sorry about the mess in your room."

C. "I put the message on your desk. I didn't know you hadn't read it."

The key to distinguishing Level 3 passive-aggressive behavior is recognizing the passive-aggressive person's lack of action regarding a problem that could otherwise be easily prevented or moderated. The person's characteristic rationalizations are the other hallmark of this level. In Chapter 11, we talk about how to confront the rationalizations and take away the satisfaction the passive-aggressive person gets by using them.

Level 4: Hidden but Conscious Revenge "I'm clever and successful"

The Level 4 (hidden but conscious revenge) passive-aggressive person makes a deliberate decision to get back at a teacher, parent, peer, or colleague by maligning his reputation, frustrating his daily life activities, or damaging and stealing objects of importance. All of these hostile acts are achieved without the other person's knowledge. Whereas Level 3 behaviors are marked by *inaction*, Level 4 behaviors are distinguished by covert but very definite *action*.

At this level, the person has hateful thoughts about her chosen target and enjoys experiencing the "sweet taste of revenge." The passive-aggressive person is keenly aware that the person with whom she is angry has enough power and authority to make her life miserable, so she decides it is not safe to confront the person openly. The Level 4 person often feels she has been mistreated, unappreciated, or discriminated against, so she feels justified in taking her secret revenge.

Level 4 behaviors could include stealing money from a stepfather's wallet, hiding a teacher's set of keys, puncturing the tires of a boyfriend's car, or planting a virus in the company's computer system. The following is an example of how the age-old behavior of passive aggression presents itself in our new age:

> Level 4: The person feels mistreated and justified in getting hidden revenge on the person she believes has slighted her.

Brandi and Tameka were best friends throughout ninth grade. Inseparable both in class and after school, their friendship hit a rift in the 10th grade, when Brandi began dating a member of the football team. Brandi started hanging out with her boyfriend and his group of friends. Tameka was jealous at first, feeling left out and abandoned by Brandi. Her feelings turned to anger when she perceived Brandi as being "too good for her." While she did not believe she had the social power or standing to directly express her feelings to Brandi, she knew how to get her message of hurt across. Using Internet sites such as MySpace and Facebook, she spread vicious rumors about her former best friend. Brandi's reputation quickly plummeted, her relationship ended, and Tameka took satisfaction in her friend's rapid fall.

The relative anonymity of the Internet is a great tool for passive-aggressive people operating at any level, from cyber-bullying to sarcastic e-mails whose biting tones can be downplayed (*I didn't mean it that way. You were reading me wrong*); we will explore this phenomenon further in Chapter 11.

Level 5: Self-Depreciation
"Getting back at you is worth the pain"

The Level 5 (self-depreciation) passive-aggressive individual is fixated on getting back at a specific person, and, to achieve these ends, he behaves in outrageously offensive and self-destructive ways that lead to his own personal rejection and alienation. The self-depreciating behaviors at this level are not as consciously motivated as those of the first four levels. They represent a pattern of pathology that will require professional intervention.

This level of self-depreciation is illustrated by the gifted student who drops out of school in her last semester and the upper-middle-class adolescent who joins a cult and dresses in bizarre and impoverished ways. While it is an adolescent trend to alter appearance in lasting ways, such as by getting tattoos or body piercings, some consciously motivated teens change their look in such a way as to bring about school suspensions, ensure employment rejection, and thoroughly horrify their parents and family.

> Level 5: This most pathological level of passive aggression involves a person who goes to self-destructive lengths to seek vengeance.

Theresa was actively involved in gymnastics from the age of 4 years all the way through high school. When her junior year grades began to drop, her parents blamed the 20+ hours a week she spent training and gave her an ultimatum: If her GPA didn't rise to at least a 3.0 after the next marking period, she would have to quit gymnastics.

Theresa dedicated extra attention to her studies and pulled two of her class averages way up. Her math grades continued to suffer, however, and her semester-ending GPA was a 2.8. Though she begged her parents for leniency and to acknowledge her improvement, they held fast to their limit. For the first time in 12 years, Theresa had to say good-bye to gymnastics.

Within the first month, Theresa gained 5 pounds. Her family and friends thought little of it, believing it to be the natural result of her reduction in exercise time. Many even commented that the extra weight suited her slender frame. In truth, the weight gain was not "natural," but rather completely intentional. As a passive-aggressive response to her parents' decision to take away gymnastics,

Theresa was purposefully packing on pounds. In her mind, she wanted to show them that by taking away this fitness-oriented pastime, they were causing her to become completely overweight and unfit. After 3 months, she had gained 25 pounds, and her once active lifestyle was now one of afterschool TV marathons and greasy foods. When 50 pounds were added to a frame that had previously never weighed more than 105 pounds, her family doctor advised her parents that Theresa was now taking on serious health risks.

Theresa's parents made a decision to reverse their suspension of gymnastics and allow their daughter to get back to the exercise program that had kept her physically healthy. When Theresa reenrolled, however, her new weight made her old routines impossible. She did not make the elite team that she had been a member of for the past 10 years and ended up quitting on her own after just 2 months.

The desire to avenge personal affronts can be overwhelming for people of all ages and personality styles. For the passive-aggressive person, who is unable or unwilling to directly express angry feelings, the need for an act or acts of vengeance may be especially strong. The passive-aggressive person is willing to damage his or her own life in dramatic and lasting ways in order to bring pain and suffering to a perceived persecutor.

Passive-Aggressive Personality Versus Passive-Aggressive Behaviors

When discussing these five levels of passive-aggressive behaviors, we are often asked, "If I use passive-aggressive behaviors, do I have a passive-aggressive personality?" This is an interesting question. Most individuals fall within the normal range of behavior and have learned a variety of ways of coping with a stressful situation. They may confront it, attack it, or withdraw from it. They may become sarcastic, regressive, humorous, dependent, reflective, or ambivalent. They may become hysterical, rational, or passive aggressive.

The obvious conclusion is that they have many ways of responding to frustrating situations, depending on the time, place, and problem. They may behave at any of the first four levels of passive-aggressive behavior, depending on the circumstances or conditions. However, when all of their passive-aggressive behaviors are added together, they represent only a small part of their total range of behavior.

This is not true for people with passive-aggressive personalities. During stressful situations, they will respond in passive-aggressive ways most of the time. For them, passive aggression is not a choice but a central part of their personality. This is the key distinction.

Summary of the Five Levels of Passive-Aggressive Behavior

In this chapter, the five levels of passive-aggressive behavior have been detailed, from the most common and least damaging to the truly pathological:

Level 1 passive-aggressive behavior pairs verbal compliance with behavioral delay. It is the most common, everyday form of the behavior and is also the one that people get away with most easily.

Level 2 passive-aggressive behavior occurs when a person complies with a given request but carries it out in an unacceptable manner. The frustrated requestor often ends up doing the task him- or herself and does not ask the person to do it again in the future.

Level 3 adds an additional layer of intention, as the passive-aggressive person uses inaction to allow a problem to escalate. He takes genuine pleasure out of watching the situation unfold and observing the anguish it causes to the target of his hidden anger.

Level 4 passive aggression occurs when a person feels justified in taking secret revenge on a person who she believes has mistreated her. The behaviors at this level reach a new level of offense, many of them even criminal.

Level 5 passive aggression surpasses anything we would consider "everyday." When a person acts in self-destructive ways that lead to his own personal rejection and alienation, his passive aggression represents a pattern of pathology that will require professional intervention.

In the next four chapters, we will use these five levels as our guide for examining passive-aggressive behaviors at school, at home, in close adult relationships, and in the workplace.

part

2

Identifying Passive-Aggressive Behaviors

Passive-Aggressive Behaviors at Home

5

Passive aggression exists in many homes and is the silent killer of healthy feelings of comfort, freedom, and intimacy among family members. Like a microscopic mite, it floats undetected in the social atmosphere of the home, contaminating the psychological comfort of everyone. No one escapes the infection of passive-aggressive behavior, because everyone develops an allergic reaction to it.

This acknowledgment of passive aggression in the home challenges the image of the middle-class family as a place of respite from the stresses of life. We believe that families at all socioeconomic levels are, in fact, battlegrounds for unexpressed feelings of anger. The "perfect family" of yesterday may be idealized fiction; in reality, the families of yesteryear were as problematic as many of the families of today. For example, Rosenfeld (1997) reported on a conference in Colonial Williamsburg by a panel of 18th-century experts who described a grim picture of family life 2 centuries ago.

> Eliza Parke Custis was whipped severely after her father removed a cottonseed she had put up her nose. She wrote in her diary, "When he put me down my proud heart swelled with anger. . . . I thought he was unjust and I felt he had degraded me."

Thomas Jefferson wrote the following to his eldest daughter, Martha, a student in Annapolis:

> If you love me, then strive to be good under every situation and to all living creatures, and to acquire those accomplishments which I have put in your power, and which will go far towards ensuring you the warmest love of your affectionate father.
> P.S. Keep my letters and read them at times, that you may always have present in your mind those things which will endear you to me.

More fascinating would be to know the types of passive-aggressive behaviors Eliza Custis and Martha Jefferson no doubt expressed toward their famous fathers. In any case, whether then or now, it is certain that passive-aggressive behavior is a pervasive and persistent household contaminant.

What makes it especially virulent is that the relationships we develop at home become our first template for interpersonal relations with the world. When a person learns to use passive-aggressive behavior at home as a first line of defense with parents, caretakers, and siblings, he learns to automatically resort to this set of behaviors with teachers, significant others, and coworkers in his world.

In this chapter, we will look at how the five levels of passive-aggressive behavior are typically manifested in the home, with an eye on how these interactions set the stage for all others.

Level 1: Temporary Compliance

The most common way of expressing passive aggression is at the first level of temporary compliance. At Level 1, the child agrees to comply with the family member's request but then fails to carry it out. Procrastination, postponement, stalling, and forgetting are typical behaviors at this level of passive-aggressive behavior.

As you read, you will no doubt find yourself familiar with the examples we give of passive-aggressive excuses and rationalizations that justify behavior. They are heard in most families. Sometimes these excuses are nothing more than garden-variety expressions of individuals who are involved in other interests, who are tired, or who perceive the request as unreasonable. The important distinction between such behavior and passive-aggressive behavior is that the latter derives from personal anger and is intended to hurt or frustrate the adult. A child at this level of passive aggression is motivated to get back at someone while justifying his or her (in)actions.

> Procrastination, postponement, stalling, and forgetting are typical Level 1 passive-aggressive behaviors.

MOM: Did you make your bed?

ASHLEIGH: Sorry! I forgot. I don't want to miss the bus. I'll do it right after school!

DAD: Did you turn the hose off?

MARY: I will, but I have to go to the bathroom first.

GRANDMOTHER: Will you come and help me now?

TODD: Sure, right after this TV show is over.

MOTHER: Come in the house now.

BILLY: I'm coming, Mom.

Billy's mother continues to call him, her voice getting louder and her mood getting darker with each summons. Billy continues to yell back that he's coming, his voice remaining steady and his mind gaining satisfaction, but his body never moving toward the door. After four requests, his mom storms outside, exasperated, yelling in front of the neighbors and appearing out of control. With feigned bewilderment, Billy plays up his role as "innocently accused child" and calmly saunters past her, into the house.

FATHER: Did you start your homework?

MATT: I will.

> That evening, Matt does everything *but* his homework. He watches TV, plays video games, talks on the phone, and IMs his friends. When his father finally loses his patience and yells at Matt, threatening to ground him, Matt turns up the volume on his iPod.

It is critical to recognize that passive aggression is initiated by parents as well as by their children. After all, what's better than a role model in developing behavioral patterns?

CHRIS: Mom, will you sign this permission slip for me?

MOM: Leave it on the counter. I'll be there in a minute.

> Chris waits and waits and becomes stressed that he is going to miss his bus and miss out on his field trip.

RICH: Dad, can you help me fix this bicycle tire?

DAD: Sure. I'm coming.

> Rich waits while his father watches the game on TV, makes a sandwich, eats it, and putters around the basement, appearing to gather tools. By the time the repair is done, Rich's friends are long gone.

Temporary Deafness

If a child is angry with an adult or irritated by a request, a passive-aggressive tactic is to feign deafness and not respond when spoken to. Many passive-aggressive individuals have learned this act of temporary deafness—a useful strategy when they do not want to do something—and use it as an enjoyable way of frustrating the adult.

DAD: Did you answer the phone?

NANCY: I didn't hear it.

MOTHER: Come to dinner. (*No response*)

MOTHER: Come to dinner! (*No response*)

MOTHER: (*Yells*) Come to dinner, Gary!

GARY: Sorry, Mom, I didn't hear you.

Temporary Blindness

Children who are passive aggressive frequently have temporary blindness when they do not want to comply with an adult's request. The pretense is an effective way of expressing one's anger while simultaneously apologizing and saying, "Oh, I'm sorry."

Mom: Are you ready for school?

Bethany: I can't find my books.

Temporary Brain Damage

A number of kids can recall with startling accuracy the statistics of every leading football player in the NFL or words to every song in a CD collection, but when it comes to carrying out a simple task that they prefer not to do, they will promptly "forget" all about it. They seem to have episodes of temporary brain damage that interfere with their ability to remember anything they do not want to do—whether it is returning a book to its owner or remembering to take out the trash, the child seems unable to remember the task. When reminded by a family member, the child is likely to respond, "Oh yes, I'll do it. It slipped my mind."

Brother: Did you bring my book back from school?

Sister: I gave it to Tom. I didn't know you wanted it back.

Mom: Did you fold the laundry?

David: I didn't know where the basket was to carry it all, so I was waiting for you to help me find it.

What is perhaps most frustrating about Level 1 passive-aggressive behavior in the home is that it happens again and again, and the child does not appear to learn from his or her experiences, regardless of the adult's criticism. With each seemingly minor act of "blindness" or procrastination, the adult becomes ever more irritated, until even the smallest act of "deafness" pushes the adult to lose control, as in the previous example of Billy and his mother. As we progress in this text and become thoroughly familiar with passive-aggressive patterns in the home, school, relationships, and workplace, we will provide you with a system for effective response to passive-aggressive behaviors that spans all levels and locations and helps prevent everyday passive-aggressive excuses from becoming long-term damaging conflicts.

Level 2: Intentional Inefficiency

Level 2 of passive-aggressive behavior occurs when a child expresses anger toward an adult by completing the request but doing it in such a way that will upset the adult, as in the following examples:

Play It Again, Sam

My mother said it was time to practice for my piano lesson, but there was a baseball game going on down the block. What kid likes to stay in and practice scales when he could be sliding into home plate? I said, "Okay," and started to play off-key and very loudly. If she was going to make me practice, I was going to irritate the heck out of her. Mother yelled, "Sammy, you know how to play better than that." I shot back, "Look, I'm doing what you asked. You have no right to get angry with me." After about 5 minutes, my mom said I could go outside and then practice the piano after supper. I learned this was a successful way of getting my way while also getting back at my mom.

Getting to the Grass Roots of the Problem

Our adolescent son, Ralph, had the responsibility of cutting the lawn on our weekend property every Saturday. One particular Saturday, he said, "Dad there is a soccer game at school. Can I have a break, and I'll cut the lawn later in the afternoon?" I felt this was an acceptable alternative, so I agreed.

Unfortunately, it rained all afternoon, so Ralph couldn't cut the lawn. The following weekend, the grass was quite high, and, being a typical father, I said to him, "Ralph, when you cut the grass today with the tractor, I want you to do a good job. I don't want you to put the tractor into high gear and cut the grass at 20 miles an hour. Since you didn't cut the grass last week and it's hot today, I want you to take your time. In fact, you may have to cut it twice to do a good job."

Clearly, he was disgusted with me and my comments. He knew how to cut the lawn and he didn't need to have me treat him like a child. He said, "You want a good job. All right, I'll give you a good job." Off he went and was on the tractor for about 2 hours. When he came into the house he was sweaty and said, "Dad, you will be happy. I cut the grass just the way you wanted, nice and neat and low."

I walked outdoors and saw about one and a half acres of dirt. I couldn't see one blade of grass. He set the lawnmower blade so low that the grass was cut to its roots. He did what I asked him to do, but in a way that made me furious.

The Joylessness of Cooking

I enjoy cooking and wanted to share this skill with my 13-year-old daughter who is in special education. One Sunday afternoon, I decided I would teach her how to make a Bundt cake, although she didn't seem interested in this culinary adventure. Stefi wanted to listen to the radio while we were baking.

I showed her how to take eggs and crack them in the bowl and how to measure out the milk, flour, and sugar. She cracked five eggs correctly, but the sixth egg missed the bowl, hit the counter, and slid down to the floor. We stopped and cleaned it up. After all, accidents do occur. She started to beat the batter by putting the bowl on her hip and stirring while dancing to the sound of the music. Inevitably, the batter started running down her leg until I couldn't stand it anymore.

Finally I exclaimed, "That's it Stefi, get out of the kitchen, you're destroying everything!" As Stefi went out the door, she stated, "Geez, Mom, how am I ever going to learn to make a Bundt cake if you don't teach me?"

There must be something about loading and unloading the dishwasher that triggers conflict between parents and kids. An uncanny number of clever variations of passive-aggressive behavior centered around this particular chore as we studied our written examples of Intentional Inefficiency:

> Charles asked his son, Nathan, to unload the dishwasher. Nathan complained that he couldn't reach the cupboard where the glasses go. Charles told him to get a chair to reach the cupboard. Nathan did not, but instead tried to place a glass on the high shelf. The glass fell and broke. Charles got upset and told Nathan that he would finish the chore. He also cleaned up the broken glass.
>
> Samantha had a chore of unloading the dishwasher once per day. After procrastinating most of the night, she began her job at 11:50 P.M., banging each dish as she picked it up and then again as she put it away. Her mother reacted to the noise with anger because she had been trying to sleep. This triggered a new round of "job definitions" to correct the late-night noise problem. Samantha interpreted the additional parameters as new territory to conquer. Every time her mother tried to box her in to prevent one problem from occurring, Samantha thought outside the box and caused a new one. Cleverly, she never disobeyed the letter of her mother's laws, though she violated the obvious spirit of every single one!

Level 3: Letting a Problem Escalate

At times, the passive-aggressive person can worsen a situation by doing nothing when he or she knows that by doing something the situation could be improved. The following examples demonstrate that a person who is passive aggressive may get pleasure out of a family member's mistake or unnecessary mishap.

Sisters Are a Girl's Worst Friend

> It was Friday evening, and it looked like I'd be sitting home watching TV. My 19-year-old sister, Suzanne, was getting ready for her date. It had been a week since we'd argued over who really owned the tights hanging in the bathroom, and she was still giving me "the silent treatment."
>
> Suzanne came downstairs to get some toothpaste and passed me in the hall, nearly knocking me over. She smiled ever so sweetly and said, "Oh, I'm sorry! I didn't see you coming!" I went into the living room to turn on the TV, trying to resign myself to the situation.
>
> "That's just great!" I thought. The TV volume was too loud! As I was pushing every button on the remote, I barely heard the telephone ringing. "This," I thought, "could be my chance to go out!"
>
> I realized the phone had been answered upstairs. I ran to it and lifted the receiver, only to hear a male voice say, "Okay, thank you." Click. Oh, no!
>
> I ran upstairs and Suzanne said, "Oh, I thought you went out for the evening. That call was for you." And then, with that sweet tone of voice, she added, "Oh, I'm so sorry."

Cinderella Has a Ball

> My stepmother and stepsister were thorns in my side throughout my high school years. One thorn in their side was my academic success. My stepmother got upset

when she saw my report cards and yelled at her daughter that she should study, like me.

Each night I sat at the kitchen table and studied, whether or not I really had homework. My stepmother often remarked how hard I studied. My stepsister and I were in the same mathematics class, but I got A's, and she was failing. Many times she'd ask me for my math homework, and I said, "Sure, here you are," with a nice, big smile. I knew that she would end up failing the course anyway, because I never showed her how to do the math. She just copied it. (Smile.)

High-Quality Child Care

I had plans on a Saturday night to go to the movies with a group of friends, but my parents forbade me to go, saying they needed me to babysit for my younger brother. They weren't even planning to pay me—they said it was one of my responsibilities within the family!

I figured that if I ever wanted to leave the house on a weekend, I would need to prove to my parents how responsible I could be. I didn't argue with them about the job, and I let my brother have a fantastic night! He got to write on the walls with his crayons, dump out all of his toys in the living room, and eat chocolate candy for dinner (and leave colorful foil wrappers around the house). I talked on the phone the whole night and kept a watchful eye on my brother, making sure he was safe and didn't get hurt in any way.

The final two examples of this level reveal instances in which a parent uses passive-aggressive means to achieve specific desired ends.

Feeding the Meter

Tanya never felt entirely comfortable with her 17-year-old daughter, Lisa, learning to drive. Lisa's driving skills were just fine, but Tanya constantly worried that Lisa would be injured in a car accident. One day, as Tanya and Lisa headed downtown to shop, Lisa skillfully parked their car on the street at a meter. She got out and filled the meter with coins, then looked at her watch and noted aloud that they had 2 hours to shop. As Tanya got out, a quick glance at the meter told her that Lisa had miscalculated and that they only had one hour to shop. Rather than adding more coins or correcting her daughter, she wordlessly joined Lisa for their shopping trip.

Two hours later, when they returned to their car, Lisa spotted the bright orange ticket tucked under her windshield wiper. The fine was $125! Lisa immediately burst into tears, knowing that she didn't have this kind of money available. Tanya hugged Lisa and reassured her that she would be willing to help with the fine. She also suggested that Lisa could save up for her share of the costs by not driving for a month, thereby saving the gas money she would have otherwise spent.

"Did you call me?"

I was wary of the new crowd my teenage son had begun to hang around. He met them at his after-school job, so they were virtual strangers to me, as opposed to his school and basketball team friends that I had gotten to know well over several years. One night, my son left his cell phone charging in the kitchen while he was in his room doing homework. The phone must have rung eight times in an hour! I didn't know how he ever got any schoolwork done with that thing buzzing. On the ninth call, I answered the phone and took a message from a hesitant girl, telling me that "everyone" was meeting at 11 p.m. at a local teen hang out. I politely thanked her and went up to my son's room. Thankfully, he was in a talkative mood and we chatted for a half an hour about basketball, after which I went straight to bed. I enjoyed our talk and knew that I was safe with an "Oh! I was coming up to give you the message but I got so caught up in your story about the game that I totally forgot" excuse, should my son find out that I took the phone call. I never felt badly about intentionally not passing on that phone message. That 30-minute conversation strengthened our relationship and just might have saved him from a risky late night out with strangers.

Passive-aggressive acts can occur out of pure anger and irritation or, as in the two previous examples, can sometimes stem from good intentions. It is important to note that, in all cases, hidden anger (at the person, at his choice of friends, at his burgeoning independence, etc.) is at the root of true passive aggression and all such acts are emotionally dishonest means of expression. While the omission of information may, in fact, have saved a young son from a dangerous night out or a teenage driver from the roads for a month, parent–child relationships do not thrive in the long run from indirect means of communication. It is important to consider how trust between parents and children—or between any people who experience a passive-aggressive dynamic—can be negatively impacted over the long run.

Level 4: Hidden but Conscious Revenge

A Level 4 passive-aggressive act is a hateful, deliberate deed. The person has angry feelings toward a sibling or parent and decides to get back at a later time in a conscious act of hostility and revenge.

Elixir of Hate

I never told anyone about what I did to my sister, Terry, about 15 years ago. Perhaps writing about this incident will relieve some of the guilt I still feel when I think about it. Terry is 2 years older than me and had it all: She was beautiful, had a great figure, did well in school, had lots of friends, and even got along with our parents. I thought she was nice to everyone but me.

One fall day, she told me Derek was taking her to a picnic at one of our local parks in Wisconsin. I thought Derek was gorgeous, and I was envious. Terry giggled and said, "Too bad you don't have a date, because this is going to be a great party."

With that comment I decided I was going to get back at her. I wondered how I could do it without her finding out. Finally, I came up with an ingenious idea. Terry would protect her beautiful skin by putting on mosquito repellent before she left. I went to the bathroom and found the bottle of repellent. I emptied half of it and filled it up with baby oil. I shook it and left it for Terry to find. Before she left, she dabbed it on her hands and face.

When she returned from her date, she was peppered with mosquito bites. She was crying and said, "I don't know what happened. It seemed like hundreds of bugs were always around me." I told her how sorry I was this had happened to her, while in my heart, I knew it was because of my lotion potion.

The Proof Was in the Stuffing

As the middle child in a family with a sister 2 years older and a brother 1 year younger, I found that I could not act out my anger directly. My sister was both physically and verbally superior to me, and my brother, though younger, was always bigger and stronger. When I was about 9, I discovered that I could get back at them in an indirect way, which I can now see was passive-aggressive behavior.

I would take some object that they used daily, such as a brush, which they normally kept in a certain place. They would go to use it, and it would have just disappeared. I would hear them mumbling to themselves, then ask my mother if she had seen it. When they asked me, I'd tell them I had no idea where they had put it.

I didn't steal the objects; I would just hide them. I enjoyed knowing I could cause them distress without accepting responsibility for it. I had forgotten how often I had used this technique until I went to college and found a pair of my sister's gloves that I had stuffed in a hole in a stuffed animal.

"You stole my mother!"

I was 14 when my parents divorced and, unlike some kids who anguish over being separated from a parent, I loved living with just my mom. It was great to have her all to myself. For 2 solid years, her focus was on me—but not in a suffocating way, like some moms'. We were best friends, and life was great!

Just after my 16th birthday, she met Joe, a teacher where I used to go to middle school. They started dating and became pretty serious pretty fast. It felt like my best friend had dumped me. Joe tried to be nice to me, but I hated him for stealing my mom away.

I did all kinds of things to try and get him to go away: stole money from his wallet, lied about my mother's birthday so he sent her flowers and balloons on the anniversary of her father's death, and even spread a few rumors around the middle school, which got him in some serious trouble with the school principal. One night, he came over for dinner and stayed way past his welcome, as far as I was concerned. While he and my mom watched TV, I snuck outside and slashed all four of his car tires.

Throughout it all, I never got caught! I was pretty clever about keeping my actions hidden, because I knew how angry my mom would be at me if she found out. That actually made me even more angry—knowing that her loyalty would be to him and that she couldn't understand how her relationship was making me feel!

Level 5: Self-Depreciation

Self-depreciation is the most serious level of passive aggression and, in most cases, represents a pathological expression of anger. The person is so angry that he or she is willing to allow him- or herself to be hurt in the process of retaliation. This form of self-abuse is a consequence of the power struggle. Moreover, the person's behaviors are so unacceptable that he or she forfeits self-esteem and the respect of his or her family members.

Unholy Revenge

My parents always had very strict rules and high expectations for me. They were big on using guilt-trips to make me feel bad if I didn't measure up to their standards. I was always really active in my church youth group and felt like this was a supportive respite for me, away from home.

After I was confirmed in the church, however, my parents started to use God against me, constantly telling me that I'd have to go to church to be forgiven for my behavior. From this time forward, church was no longer my sanctuary. I started out by wearing all black clothing to mass, including studded wristbands and earrings. I prayed too loudly and sung hymns off-key. When my youth-group leader took me aside to ask about my erratic behavior, I told him that I hated him and hated God.

Afterwards, I hated myself for having said such awful things to the one person who had always been there for me—but to take it back would have been to give in to my parents, and I couldn't bring myself to do that at the time. I was perfectly willing to suffer the alienation from this once-important part of my life because no matter how badly it made me feel, I knew it made my parents feel even worse!

Fired!

I was in foster care from the age of 6 and lived with many families over the years—some good, some not so good. Likewise, I had been passed around to many foster care caseworkers and knew that some cared for me a lot more than others. When Jenna came into my life, I thought things would really turn around for me. She was young, smart, intuitive, and great at her job as my caseworker. For 3 years, she really helped me out a lot, finding loving families and making sure I could attend good schools.

I had just been placed with a new family when Jenna announced to me that she was interviewing for a promotion at work. If she got the new job, she wouldn't be my caseworker anymore, though she promised she'd keep in touch. I'd heard that one before! I couldn't believe she was so willing to abandon me, just for a few more bucks in her paycheck.

The new family I was with was awful. The mother did drugs right in front of me and the other foster kids, and the father was violent when he drank. I suffered quite a bit during the 4 months I was there—the mother asked me to buy drugs for her, the foster father hit me and the other kids whenever we did anything wrong, and I never saw any of the money that was supposed to be for my school supplies or clothing. When Jenna would check in on me by phone, I would tell her that everything was fine.

She kept me updated on her life, too, including her transition to the new position. The day before she was to start her new job, I cut school and took a bus to the foster care office. I found my way to her supervisor's office and knocked on his door. With a bruised and swollen eye from my foster father's latest rampage, I laid out the details of how I had suffered over the last 4 months at the hands of my foster family.

Jenna took the fall for not having checked in on me adequately. Not only did she not get the promotion, but she was fired from the agency entirely. Before she left, she tried to ask me why I hadn't been honest with her about the abuse I had faced in the foster home, but I was still too angry to speak with her. In my mind, every punch I took was worth her losing her job and being punished for leaving me.

"Look who I brought home!"

Addison felt like she had been under her parents' thumb for her entire life. As a child, she knew that her classmates were allowed to play unsupervised after school, though her own mother always insisted on being in the same room when any of her friends came over. As a teenager, Addison was not allowed to date, nor would her parents permit her to have a job in the summers or after school. They felt very strongly about protecting her from "bad influences."

When Addison was 18, she moved out of her parents' home, much to their dismay. At 19, she dropped out of community college, and at 20, she was pregnant. She quickly married the father of her child, a boy she had known for only a month. Though Addison could not wait to get away from her hometown just 2 years earlier, she seemed to take joy in returning to her parents' home and showing off her new family to the one she had left behind.

"Don't leave me!"

Ellen was a single mother of two teenage children. The older son had already left home for college, and the younger one, Jason, was a junior in high school. When Jason began talking about the college admissions process and asking to visit schools, Ellen was faced with a thought that terrified her—being alone. Over the course of Jason's 11th- and 12th-grade school years, Ellen tried every passive-aggressive trick in the book—forgetting her meetings with his college counselor, sending applications in late, not telling Jason about important deadlines, and throwing away mail sent by universities.

Two months before Jason was to leave home to attend a university 90 miles from home, Ellen began binge drinking. Night after summer night, Jason would find empty liquor bottles and discover his mother either passed out or heavily intoxicated. The young and vulnerable child had no idea how to care for her or what to do when he found her. It did occur to him, after the fifth consecutive evening of finding her like this, that maybe he should not leave her alone in the coming months.

Summary

In Chapter 2, we discussed the four developmental pathways most commonly traveled by individuals who develop passive-aggressive personalities. These shared histories provide strong support for our belief that a passive-aggressive personality style has its roots in the home. With passive aggression as the template for significant interpersonal relationships, a person becomes preprogrammed to use this set of behaviors across many stressful situations—with teachers, in relationships, and toward coworkers throughout his or her life.

In the next chapter, we examine passive-aggressive behavior within school settings—the place where children spend the next largest percentage of their time during their formative years.

Passive-Aggressive Behaviors at School

Public education for students, like the military, is organized as a top-down administrative system. Each member of the school system has a designated rank, responsibility, role, and function. This administrative pecking order is the standard and accepted way of operating in a school system. The superintendent has the most authority and power to manage and control the educational system. He or she delegates specific responsibilities to the assistant superintendent, supervisors, principals, teachers, and classroom aides in a descending stair-step order. All of these adults, however, have more power and status than do the students.

Students are placed in a virtually powerless role in most school systems. If they are to succeed academically, they must accept their roles as compliant to the authority of the teacher and his or her classroom values, standards, and rules. Students also must be motivated to learn and have the prerequisite skills to attend class and respond to the classroom lesson quickly and quietly. Most of all, they need to be able to control their daily frustrations in the classroom without becoming behavior problems for the teacher.

In our observation of classrooms and in consultation with teachers and principals, teachers who are authoritarian or perfectionistic most frequently encourage the development of situational passive-aggressive behavior in students.

The Authoritarian Teacher

The classroom teacher is the primary authority figure for students. He or she has the responsibility of teaching the assigned curriculum and objectives of the grade level. The teacher's personality and the social atmosphere he or she creates in the classroom have a profound influence on a student's attitudes, feelings, and behaviors.

> I have come to a frightening conclusion. I am the decisive element in the classroom. It is my personal approach that creates the climate. It is my daily mood that makes the weather. As a teacher, I possess tremendous power to make a child's life miserable or joyous. I can be a tool of torture or an instrument of inspiration. I can humiliate or humor, hurt or heal. In all situations, it is my response that decides whether a crisis will be escalated or de-escalated and a child humanized or de-humanized. (G. H. Ginott, 1975, p. 163)

If a classroom teacher is authoritarian, has perfectionistic and unreasonable standards, focuses on negative student behavior, and actively punishes students who deviate from his or her expectations, the teacher sets the psychological conditions for students to learn passive-aggressive ways of relating. We have observed a few teachers who fit this profile. We also have observed students who are not typically passive aggressive but who become passive aggressive as a way of coping with a demanding, authoritarian, perfectionistic teacher.

In our experience, teachers seem to have little awareness of the dynamics of a passive-aggressive student. While schools usually have long lists of policies and procedures for managing overtly aggressive behavior, and teachers receive much professional education and in-service training related to minimizing classroom disruptions, there is little out there (as our literature search confirmed) to equip teachers with skills to recognize and effectively manage the indirect expression of anger, such as in passive aggression.

Teachers find it irritating and confusing that a nonaggressive student can cause them to experience such feelings of anger over time. They have described to us again and again how they have "had it" with such students and how they can no longer even look at them without feeling animosity.

Passive-aggressive students master the art of emotional concealment by hiding their anger behind a mask of annoying and confusing behaviors. Without proper knowledge and understanding, it can be difficult for authority figures in the classroom to see beyond frustrating behaviors and to identify underlying feelings of anger. Once a teacher is aware of the dynamics of passive aggression and has a strong working knowledge of the five levels of this behavior, he or she becomes well equipped to recognize it quickly and early on, in its less damaging forms. With early detection comes emotional neutrality, allowing the teacher to rationally manage his or her responses and to successfully connect with the passive-aggressive student.

Passive-Aggressive Behavior in the Classroom

In this chapter, typical passive-aggressive behaviors of students are described. Examples were selected from stories provided by our seminar participants to illustrate the successful passive-aggressive ways in which students can frustrate their teachers and teachers can frustrate their students. The discussion is divided into the five levels of passive-aggressive behavior we discussed in Chapter 4. Passive-aggressive students are not restricted to any one of the tactics described. The skilled passive-aggressive student uses a variety of techniques to get the teacher stirred up emotionally.

Level 1: Temporary Compliance

This level of passive-aggressive behavior occurs when a student is asked by an adult to carry out a specific task that he or she does not want to do at the time. Instead of resisting, the student agrees to do it, but then delays or does not do it at all.

Temporary Blindness

"I can't see it"

Gary is a student in my fourth-grade class. When I ask him to do something in class, he rarely says no. Most of the time he agrees to do it, but then doesn't. One day, I asked Gary if he would walk to the bookshelf at the back of the classroom and bring me the encyclopedia lettered M. Gary nodded, but he didn't seem happy. He slowly walked over to the shelf and said, "I don't see it!" I told him that he was looking at the top shelf instead of the middle shelf. He replied, "It's still not here." I asked him if he could find the W, pull it out of the bookcase, and see if it was the M placed upside down. Gary looked for a few minutes, turned and said, "It's not there." By this time I was so frustrated, I walked toward Gary and from about 8 feet away I spotted the M volume. I looked at him in a disgusted way and said, "There it is." He replied, "Oh, I didn't see it!"

Temporary Deafness

"Can you hear me now?"

Karen is in my ninth-grade math class. She is well behaved and smart, but occasionally I have noticed that she seems not to hear me when I call on her. Yesterday I wrote a simple equation on the board. I noted that Karen was not paying attention, so I asked her to solve it. She did not respond, so I repeated her name a second time. Still, she did not look up or answer. By this time I was angry and yelled, "Karen!" She looked up and said meekly, "Are you calling me?" "Yes," I replied sternly. Karen smiled, "Oh, I'm sorry. I didn't hear you. What is it you'd like me to do?" I was so upset, I replied, "Just forget it. I'll ask a student who is paying attention."

"I'll take the Fifth Amendment"

Up until the fifth grade, I was a model student and many times the teacher's pet, but when I entered fifth grade, I felt that my teacher did not like me, so I disliked her. She always wrote on my report card that I talked too much, was a social butterfly, and never finished my work. I couldn't understand why she didn't like me. I remember clearly deciding that I would never talk to her again unless she initiated the conversation. I would also pretend not to hear her until she asked me twice. I know that my behavior upset her, but what she didn't know was how much I enjoyed not talking to her.

Temporary Brain Damage

It's Showtime!

Dan was a bright, musically talented piano student to whom I taught weekly private lessons. Week after week he came to his lesson thoroughly unprepared; he would forget to bring his sheet music, not be able to recall which piece he had chosen for a recital, and mess up on even the most fundamental scales. I cringed at the thought of his upcoming recital, where he would play alongside my most dedicated, hardworking students. I was embarrassed for Dan, who would have to play in front of his parents and peers, and for myself as well, because his inabilities would reflect poorly on my instruction. I considered not letting him perform, but I didn't want to humiliate him in this way.

When the day of the recital came, I was floored by Dan's performance. It was flawless! The best of any of my students! What I realized years later was that Dan's performance during our private lessons was his way of letting me know that he didn't like the step-by-step structure of my lesson; he found it confining to his creativity and self-expression. His dismal one-on-one behavior and dazzling public performance were nothing less than his passive-aggressive way of showing me what he thought of my teaching atmosphere!

The Art of Procrastination and the Skill of Dawdling

Many passive-aggressive students have perfected the art of procrastination, or completing any assigned task with unnecessary slowness. They do not feign temporary blindness, deafness, or brain damage. They agree to do the assigned task but then dawdle, mess around, and delay completing the task as long as possible. The modus operandi seems to be, *When I'm upset at the adult, never do anything today that I might consider doing tomorrow.* When the teacher confronts them about their behavior, they make endless and emotional promises to make up all of the unfinished work and to complete the assignment. However, they become creative and clever in devising excuses to explain why they were unable to meet their promises. Teaching one of these students can be an irritating experience for teachers.

"If I only had more patience"

I was taking my sixth-grade class to the library. All of the students were in line and ready to go except Eric, a student who is mainstreamed in my class. Eric was still at his desk, so I said, "Eric, come on. Let's get going!" Eric gave me that classical answer, "I'm coming." I thought that perhaps Eric was mad at me, because earlier that morning I told him to quit goofing around and to attend to his work. Instead of lining up with his class, he started to pick up all of the paper under his desk, behavior that would have been appropriate 10 minutes earlier but was totally inappropriate now. Next, he walked over to the pencil sharpener and began to empty it. By then, I was fuming. Eric was holding up the entire class, and I seemed to be tolerating it. Finally, I'd had it, and yelled, "Eric, come now! Come this very second!" Eric looked surprised and said, "You know if you would have waited one half of a second more, I was coming. My foot was in the air, so you didn't have to yell at me. I was only trying to clean up." After I took the class to the library, I began to doubt my own ability. Perhaps I should have been more patient. Maybe I should be more tolerant. And maybe I did overreact. After all, Eric was cleaning up the classroom.

Level 2: Intentional Inefficiency

Level 2 passive-aggressive behavior occurs when a student is unwilling to

> In Level 2, intentional inefficiency, the student expresses anger by completing the assigned task in a manner and at a quality level that are certain to upset the teacher.

do work or is just plain angry with a teacher for some previous incident. Once again, the student is not being openly resistant to the teacher's request. The student cannot be accused of not doing the assignment. This protects the student from being identified as oppositional while also providing the opportunity to get back at the teacher behind a mask of inefficiency.

The Painful Hello

Tony was an adolescent in our school who had strong negative feelings toward authority figures—especially me, the principal. Each morning, I walked through the corridors and met the students when the school buses arrived. If Tony saw me, he would come up to me, say "Good morning," and simultaneously punch me on the shoulder. His punch was just hard enough that I knew it wasn't friendship, but it wasn't too hard, either. I knew if I tried to call Tony on this behavior, he would say, "Hey, Big Man, I was just trying to be friendly. I don't know why you're making such a big deal out of saying 'hello.'" Thinking about this, I decided to set new boundaries with Tony. I said to him, "I appreciate your wanting to say 'hello' to me, but let's do it in a different way. When you see me, I want you to stop, say 'Good morning,' and stick out your hand. I will stop, say 'Good morning, Tony,' and stick out my hand. Then we will shake hands like gentlemen." I asked him to repeat what I'd said to make sure we both knew the procedure. The next day, I met Tony in the corridor. He walked over, stopped, and said, "Hello." I stopped and said, "Good morning, Tony." As we were shaking hands, he stepped on my toes. He immediately apologized, but I noticed a small grin on his face. Tony had just demonstrated the dynamics of passive-aggressive behavior. We were shaking hands, an act of friendship, while he was stepping on my toes, an act of hostility.

Cleaning Up in Class

Mr. Brown asked Myra to water the classroom plants. In the process, Myra managed to knock a plant off the windowsill, spill water on the floor, accidentally hit another pupil with the broom while sweeping up the plant debris, bump into a classmate who was painting, and step on the toes of a shy student on her way to the teacher's desk. Finally, Mr. Brown shouted, "Myra, I never want you to help me again!" "Gee, Mr. Brown, I was just trying to do what you wanted me to do and clean up our room," Myra replied.

Math Time

I'm a special education teacher and take pride in my ability to reeducate troubled students. For 90% of the students, I am a successful teacher, but when it comes to Claude, nothing seems to work. I can't explain why he upsets me or why I get so frustrated when I try to help him.

The incident began when Claude raised his hand and said that he was having some trouble with his math story problems. He asked me for help. I said I would be happy to help, and he asked me to read the first problem to him. As I started to read, I noticed that Claude started staring at the ceiling. When I asked him what he was doing, he said that he was staring at the ceiling because it helped him think better. I asked him to do me a favor and to try thinking as he was silently reading the math problem. He replied, "Sure thing, no problem." He asked me to read the same problem a second time, and while I was reading it, Claude was rocking back and forth in his chair. I reached out and put my hand on the back of his chair and said, "Claude, please keep the four legs of your chair on the floor." He replied, "Sure thing, Teach, no problem." He asked me to read the same problem a third time. By now I was getting angry and said, "I want you to pay attention. This is the last time I'm going to read this to you." I read, and Claude started making clicking noises with his tongue while also tapping a pencil on his desk. Finally, I said, "Claude, that's it! I'm not helping you now or in the future, until you pay attention." Claude smirked and said, "But Teach, that's the reason why I'm in your special ed class." As I left him, I felt like tearing out my hair.

One Eye Open

Trenton, who has a learning disability, was a member of our school tumbling group. Mr. Salinas, his gym teacher, had arranged for a special practice session that was scheduled to take place at the same time I was to meet with Trenton for his weekly remedial reading session. This reading session had priorities over other school activities and could not be rescheduled. Trenton did not tell me about his tumbling practice, and I was unaware that Trenton wanted very much to be with his team.

When Trenton entered my office, he seemed rather sluggish. I had organized a very exciting and helpful lesson for him. When I gave Trenton the assignment and asked him to read, I was surprised by his behavior. As he started to read, he put his right hand over his right eye. When I asked him why he was doing this, he replied, "I am learning to read with my left eye in case I injure my right eye." I told him to put his hand down and to stop playing around. Trenton looked at me, dropped his right hand, and then put his left hand over his left eye and continued to read. I was so annoyed by his behavior and so disappointed that my wonderful lesson would never be appreciated that I said to him, "Trenton, that's it. No more remedial reading for you. I want you to go back to your class." Trenton grinned and said, "Thank you very much." I didn't understand his behavior until I later learned that he immediately went to his tumbling session.

These examples of passive-aggressive behaviors illustrate just some of the many ways students can use intentional inefficiency to get back at an authority figure in a school setting. Still others abound:

- Some students frustrate teachers by talking slowly or quietly. The teacher asks them a question, and their reply is so halting and meandering that the teacher says impatiently, "Come on, speed it up! Cut to the action!" Or, "Speak a little louder; we can't hear you."

- Another passive-aggressive tactic is to respond to the teacher's comment in a concrete manner, causing the other students to laugh. The teacher says, "I want everyone in this class to be quiet as a mouse." Johnny replies, "Squeak, squeak, squeak!" Or the teacher might say, "Cut it out!" and Melissa says, "Cut, cut, cut, cut, cut," making a scissors motion with her hand.

- A third-grade teacher reported an incident with Larry when she read a story about farm animals. When she came to the name of an animal, Larry made the sound of that animal. This caused the other students to join him, so Larry was reprimanded. He replied, "I thought I was being helpful and you wanted me to show the class how the animals sounded."

A key to passive aggression and the hallmark of this particular level is that students conceal their anger beneath a mask of compliance. Whether it be instigating peers to make disruptive animal sounds or trashing a classroom, it is all done under the clever guise of being helpful. Therefore, when the teacher overtly expresses anger or exasperation over the behavior, the student can feign shock, surprise, and even hurt that the teacher would so misconstrue his or her deeds.

Passive-aggressive students are masters at afflicting others while claiming to be the afflicted. This is what makes their behavior complete—first they succeed in getting others to act out their own hidden anger, and then they fuel this exposed anger by acting like an innocently accused victim.

Level 3: Letting a Problem Escalate

In Level 3 passive-aggressive behavior, the student expresses anger at the teacher by making a conscious decision not to act when such action would have prevented a problem from occurring.

Keys to Success

I must have been 13 or 14 years old when this incident happened in my high school art class. I always thought of myself as a better-than-average art student, and many of my friends would compliment me on how unusual and creative my artwork was. This particular period, Mrs. Brandis was returning our midsemester art projects, and I was eagerly awaiting my grade. When I looked at my grade, I was upset. I received a C when I was sure I deserved at least a B. I remember thinking that Mrs. Brandis didn't like me and that she'd given me this low grade not because of my art project, but because she thought I was too spunky.

I was still sulking later in the period when I noticed that Mrs. Brandis' set of keys had fallen into an open drawer as she was cleaning up the art table. I knew they were the keys to her kingdom, but I decided not to say anything. At the end of the art period, Mrs. Brandis started looking for her keys. When she couldn't find them, she panicked and asked everyone in the class to look for them. She kept on explaining how important they were and how they must be found. Ten minutes later they were still lost, and Mrs. Brandis was distraught. She said she didn't know what she would do, since she wouldn't be able to drive home, and she had to take care of her elderly mother.

Finally, I felt I had enjoyed watching her "stew in her own juices" long enough. I quietly mentioned that the last time I saw her keys they were on the art table. We walked over and she started moving the jars and piles of paper around. I started to open the drawers, and much to my amazement, I found her keys in the third drawer. Mrs. Brandis could not thank me enough. She was most appreciative, and I remember getting A's on all my art projects the rest of the semester.

We would be remiss if we did not include examples of situations in which teachers frustrate students through passive-aggressive behaviors. It is certain that two can play at this game, and it is also true that passive-aggressive kids grow up to be passive-aggressive adults who use these behaviors wherever they go. In the next two examples, we will look at teachers who exhibit Level 3 behaviors in their classrooms.

"It says so right here in the syllabus"

At the beginning of each unit, I give my eighth-grade social studies class a mini-syllabus that outlines the reading assignments and test dates for the material. I want my students to be familiar with the high school system of more independent responsibility for coursework. At the same time, I realize that my students are still young kids who benefit from reminders, so I make it a practice to announce homework on a daily basis and remind students of upcoming tests a week in advance.

When one of my students, Justin, received what I considered to be an unnecessary pass to be late to my class every Monday, I decided I would let him learn the hard way how important it was to get to class on time. I made it a point to issue all of my announcements and reminders at the beginning of class. Students were fully informed of anything that was due for the week and of what would be covered on the next test. Anyone who was late simply missed out.

When Justin walked into class one test day, I watched his face turn white. He approached my desk, telling me that he didn't know about the test and hadn't studied the material. I could tell he was worried. I took out a copy of the mini-syllabus and pointed out the test date, reminding him that it was his responsibility to keep up with the schedule and be responsible for anything he missed when not in class. Justin walked to his seat, defeated. He failed the test and brought his overall average from a B to a C+.

When the principal asked me about the hard line I had taken with Justin, I explained my black-and-white policy, showing him the syllabus. What I didn't share was how I'd offered reminders to other students and had left Justin out intentionally. Looking back, I realize I was getting back at Justin for his excused lateness, which I had taken as a personal affront to my teaching.

In this example, Justin seemed to accept his relatively powerless position and did not argue in the moment about the fairness of the teacher's actions. Our hope would be that he did learn a lesson about keeping track of assignments and dates—maybe he even went out that night and bought a personal date planner! With many kids, however, such silent acquiescence would not be the case.

Some kids would be openly aggressive in class, shouting at the teacher, slamming schoolbooks, and kicking over a trash can on the way back to their seat. Some might cry. Still others—children who tend toward passive-aggressive behaviors—might wordlessly accept their fate to take the test unprepared, but would wait for their next opportunity to up the ante and exact another round of revenge on the teacher. Violence begets violence, and passive aggression begets passive aggression; this is the phenomenon of *counter–passive aggression* that we defined in Chapter 1. In the next example, we'll take a look at a teacher who exhibits Level 3 counter–passive aggression in response to a student's hidden anger.

Permission Slip

Christopher always came to class unprepared. He could keep up as far as the subject matter was concerned, but when it came to having pencils sharpened or enough paper to take notes, he was constantly interrupting class to borrow supplies. Most days, I saw this as Christopher's way of getting attention. Some days, I felt like this was his intentional way of getting under my skin. There was no way I was going to let this kid make me lose my cool.

On the morning of a field trip, Christopher let me know that he couldn't find his permission slip. Rather than helping him look or sending him to the office to call his mother, I informed him that he could spend the day in in-school suspension. When this didn't seem like such a bad option to him, I reminded him that not going on the field trip would impact his participation grade and that he would have to attend Saturday detention as well. This got his attention. Saving face was everything to Christopher, but with my escalation of the consequences on top of my lack of action to secure permission for him for the trip, he fell apart right in front of the class. I felt a little bad watching him cry, but I also felt justified that if he had been more prepared, he never would have had a problem.

In Chapter 9, we will review this phenomenon of counter–passive aggression in greater detail.

Level 4: Hidden but Conscious Revenge

In Level 4 passive-aggressive behavior, the student has hostile feelings toward the teacher and consciously decides to get hidden revenge at a later time. Examples of hidden revenge can range in seriousness from undercover insults to criminal behavior. In all of the cases, the student is angry with the teacher and expresses that anger behind the teacher's back. The goal in the first two (less serious) examples is not to hurt the teacher but to make fun of him while winning group support.

The Tongue

I remember being angry with my English teacher and sticking my tongue out at her as she passed. My classmates saw me do this and laughed. When the teacher turned around, we all looked angelic.

The Finger

My physical education teacher was always telling us to do more push-ups, chin-ups, and knee bends than I could do. One time I was so ticked by his escalating demands that I gave him the finger gesture behind his back. Several of my classmates smiled at me. Without any verbal exchange, I felt vindicated.

In all cases at this level, the student believes that a teacher deserves to pay a price for a perceived insult or act of disrespect. In the following two examples, the Level 4 passive-aggressive student derives genuine pleasure from watching or hearing about how the teacher has suffered.

Indiana Joan and the Desk of Doom

A prim and proper first-year English teacher treated me badly all year long. When handing out spelling tests, she often said, "Well, Wendy, I see you failed again." I caught two garden snakes on my farm and brought them to school. Before my teacher entered the classroom one morning, I placed them in the top center drawer of her desk. Just as class was getting ready to begin, she reached in that drawer for her pen. I couldn't wait for her reaction. Oh boy! I swear her feet did not touch the floor as she fled from that classroom. Whenever I think about it, I still laugh. Most important, I never got caught.

Farewell to Grades

I felt that my 10th-grade science teacher, Mr. Patton, had it in for me. He always assigned me to work with the least knowledgeable student in the class, even though he knew I was very motivated to achieve. One day, after I turned in my lab report, Mr. Patton confronted me and said that because I allowed my partner to copy the report, he was going to drop my grade one letter. This made me furious, but I felt I could do nothing about it.

The following week, as we were leaving his class, I noticed that Mr. Patton's grade book was at the edge of his desk. As I walked by it, I gave it a nudge and it dropped it off his desk and into the wastebasket. I later heard that he was seething with frustration about losing his grade book for all his classes. I remember how much I enjoyed hearing about this catastrophe.

The Basics of Web-Site Design

Mandy loved computers but hated her computer teacher. She perceived him as rude when he directed her to stay on task with her classmates instead of moving ahead at her own pace. After studying the basics of Web-site design in class, Mandy decided on a perfect way to show her teacher how much she actually could stay on a task. She built a small Web site dedicated to him. Using a real photo from the yearbook and tons of false, embarrassing information, she published the site online and anonymously publicized it around the school. Her teacher was humiliated in front of the student body and had to defend himself against the untrue postings when confronted by school administrators. Mandy enjoyed the drama from her safe distance. Recognizing the impact of this first Web site, she realized the potential for building others related to classmates she did not favor . . .

Level 5: Self-Depreciation

Self-depreciation is the most serious level of passive aggression, and it is beyond the range of a situational reaction. This level of passive-aggressive behavior is a pathological way of expressing anger—most often to parents, but sometimes to teachers as well. The behaviors are so unacceptable or repulsive that the student depreciates himself in the process. While the student may win the power struggle, he loses self-esteem, respect from others, and possibly his academic future.

Motivated to Fail

I have been teaching advanced English in high school for years, but I had never had a student in my class like Alfred. At first, I thought Alfred was the perfect student. He was intelligent and well read, participated freely in the group discussions, and wrote with unusual fluency and insight for his age. I even felt that Alfred liked me. But when it came to taking my exams, he was sure to receive a low grade. His answers to the test questions were incomplete, fragmented, and sketchy. I wondered if he had test anxiety, but when I observed him taking my exam, he seemed relaxed and comfortable. After Alfred received a C– midsemester grade, I asked him to see me during his study hall to discuss my concerns about his low test grades. As we talked about his underachievement, he said that he wasn't interested in grades but only in knowledge. He felt he was learning a lot in my class. I tried to convince him he could have high grades and knowledge, but there was no change in Alfred's test scores for the rest of the semester. His class participation saved him from failing, but I was unable to give him an A, which he could have achieved easily.

The following semester, the school psychologist told me she had met with Alfred's parents, and they had decided to transfer him to a private school. The father was particularly upset because he had plans for Alfred to attend Princeton, and he was alarmed that his son would not get in if his grades did not improve. The psychologist was certain that Alfred was in a passive-aggressive battle with his father, and Alfred seemed more motivated to fail and win the battle than to achieve and please his father.

Hitting the Fan

Tom was one of the most complicated 11-year-old students I ever taught. He was bright, attractive, and sullen. He rarely smiled, reached out to his peers, or showed any interest in the world around him. I was told that he was physically abused and emotionally disturbed and currently was living with his aunt and uncle. One day in my classroom, his problem—as the saying goes—hit the fan.

Tom was not paying attention to my instructions, so I stopped, called his name, and gave him a warning. A few minutes later I noticed he had his head down on his desk, so I interrupted the class and told him that he had better pay attention and finish his work or he would have to stay in during recess. My reprimand must have made Tom angry. He gave me a frozen stare and put his head down on the desk again. I told the class to ignore him, because Tom would just sit there until he finished his assignment.

Ten minutes later, one of the students said, "What's that smell!? Something stinks in here!" The odor was putrid and reeked throughout the room. The students were gagging, and, as I looked at Tom, I knew. He had defecated in his pants and sat there without any sense of discomfort. When I asked him if he had had an accident, he replied, "Yes," followed by a smirk. The message was clear. Tom got back at me. He seemed to have more pleasure causing me some discomfort than he did suffering any embarrassment for soiling himself in the classroom.

Dressed for Success

I teach at Southgate, a high school in the suburbs of Chicago. Southgate is known for its academic programs and number of merit scholarship winners. The school staff and administration are supportive, and the students are highly motivated to succeed. It is an honor to be on the staff of this school.

When I met my 10th-grade English class for the first time, I was surprised by the appearance of Donna. She had a black biker's jacket, tattered jeans, a dreadlock hairdo, and several body tattoos; her fingernails were black painted. She looked like a member of a delinquent gang. The girls in my class found her difficult to accept and reported some of her upsetting comments, such as, "I'm a member of a devil-worshiping cult," and "Jews and blacks are destroying our country."

I was expecting Donna to be vocal and oppositional. Instead, she was quiet and conforming. Her behavior and test scores were inconsistent but acceptable.

One Monday morning she came to class and refused to do anything. I gave her several options, but nothing seemed to work. Finally, I asked her to leave and see her counselor, which she did without any fuss. Later, I heard her mother was coming to a school conference about Donna, and I asked to attend. When Donna's mother arrived and was introduced to the staff, I was shocked by her appearance. She was the absolute opposite of Donna. She looked like she had stepped out of a fashion magazine, or perhaps like the stereotype of the wealthy society woman raising money for the Chicago Symphony.

When Donna entered the room and sat next to her mother, there was no possibility that anyone would guess they were related. The mother started to apologize for Donna's appearance, saying, "Donna and I have real problems. She seems to do everything she can to upset me. I've asked her a hundred times not to wear these clothes, but she wears them anyway. No wonder she doesn't have any friends or success in school."

When Donna was asked to talk about school, she said, "It's alright. I have no complaints." The counselor recognized that Donna was angry with her mother and was getting back at her by dressing and behaving this way.

In each of these examples of self-depreciation, it is clear that the student's issues are rooted in something much more profound and chronic than simple teacher conflict or academic difficulty. Though Level 5 passive aggression often spills over into school, relationships, and even adult workplace settings, this kind of pathological self-depreciation almost always has its roots in a child's home.

Some acts of self-depreciation that are readily apparent in the home and school are also things that may, at first, fit the profile of typical adolescent behavior, such as the following:

- multiple piercings
- multiple tattoos
- unusual clothing
- academic failing
- loss of after-school job
- drug and alcohol use
- promiscuous behavior
- unsafe driving habits

The distinction between normal and passive-aggressive behavior is the degree and intensity of the behavior. It might be common for young people to get a tattoo or even multiple tattoos, but when a person chooses to cover his or her body with offensive artwork or in such a way that turns off interviewers, the behavior may be a signal of self-depreciation. Likewise, multiple piercings, substance abuse, reckless driving—anything that could initially pass as normal adolescent experimentation—may in fact be a passive-aggressive person's way of acting out his or her troubled inner feelings.

When children travel on a pathway to passive aggression from an early age and never learn to accept or effectively express angry feelings, self-destructive behavior reflects their private turmoil. At this most serious level, it is no longer believable to shrug off the acts of self-harm or justify the behaviors as "a stage." Rather, students who are willing to cause serious, lasting harm to themselves through passive-aggressive acts of self-depreciation need adults to recognize their behavior for what it is. The ability to hear their call from amidst the noise of their behavior could be critical in preventing further, riskier self-depreciation from occurring.

Summary

In Chapters 5 and 6, we have explored the ways in which passive-aggressive behavior shows up in kids at home and in school. We also took a sneak peek at the phenomenon of counter–passive aggression and acknowledged that adult behavior is central to fueling or squashing passive aggression. In the next two chapters, we will take a look at life further down the passive-aggressive pathway. What takes place within marital relationships when passive-aggressive patterns have been ingrained in a person's behavioral repertoire from an early age? How does a passive-aggressive person fare in the workplace? Real-life scenarios will be examined to understand how passive aggression plays out in adulthood, and, in the final chapters, we discuss how to break the cycle of passive-aggressive conflict for all age groups.

Passive-Aggressive Behaviors in Marriage and Extended Family

While passive-aggressive behavior may be characteristic of certain stages of child and adolescent development, it is most certainly not a pattern that limits itself to youth. Adults exhibit passive aggression for the same reasons and at the same distinct levels as the children and adolescents we've studied thus far. Like the younger cohorts we looked at in Chapters 5 and 6, adults who use passive aggression may do so situationally or chronically, in ways that are easily justified or in a manner that is hard to excuse. In all age groups, the behavior is about the phenomenon of hidden anger and the toll it takes on interpersonal relationships across a wide range of settings.

Although defensive behavior such as passive aggression is a predictable outcome of specific developmental pathways and may even serve to protect an individual during childhood from abusive, dysfunctional family dynamics, its usefulness does expire. Patterned passive aggression rarely serves an adult well. Yet, early habits are the hardest to break. Because chronically passive-aggressive people tend to overgeneralize and respond to anyone they perceive as hostile, as if they were the abusive adults from their earliest encounters, even trustworthy family members and genuinely loved partners may become targets of their passive aggression. These bystanders rarely do anything to elicit anger but rather unwittingly represent an authority figure that the passive-aggressive person has become developmentally preprogrammed to passively resist. The phenomenon of passive-aggressive behavior among adults is particularly harmful for exactly this reason; its victims are often undeserving of the anger that is directed toward them and are especially hurt, confused, and frustrated when they receive it.

Another aspect that makes adult passive aggression particularly toxic is how often it is modeled by those who witness it. Children of passive-aggressive parents learn these patterns as a way of life, believing that hiding anger is the right, healthy, proper thing to do. Spouses of passive-aggressive individuals learn that the way to relate is through silence, resentment, and doing less when asked for more. This chapter focuses on passive-aggressive behavior between spouses and extended family.

How Excessive Civility Blocks Intimacy

In Chapter 2, we explored the four developmental pathways to passive aggression. Here, we elaborate on how these pathways may lead a person to struggle with closeness in adult relationships.

If an adult was raised in fear of the open expression of anger, whether because it might provoke retaliation from an abusive adult or because it would be an indication of the child's innate badness and would violate standards of goodness and social approval, then his or her communication channels within a relationship will be affected. If a child learns that passive aggression is an effective and satisfying way of getting back at a domineering parent or coping with perceived personal inadequacies, then that child's closest relationships are likely characterized by pleasant exteriors marred by a distinct lack of intimacy.

> Todd and Bridget have been married for 6 years. Both describe their marriage as "good," yet would agree privately that their marriage lacks intimacy. Todd was raised in a home in which anger was never acknowledged. As an adult, he remains emotionally unexpressive. This frustrates and disappoints Bridget to no end, because she believes Todd should be available to satisfy all of her emotional needs. This irrational belief of Bridget's creates an expectation that is impossible to achieve in their marriage. It isolates them from their friends and family and creates a reservoir of unexpressed feelings of anger.
>
> Both feel powerless to talk about the irritating behaviors they experience because any discussion of a spouse's behavior might upset the other person. More importantly, they are unlikely to talk about their own wants and emotional needs. Unable to express their feelings, they falsely tolerate each other's angry attitudes and behaviors. Their compromise is to be polite to each other and to express their anger in passive-aggressive ways. Theirs is the "civilized" way of avoiding intimacy.

When passive aggression blocks intimacy between parents, it also provides a dysfunctional model of self-expression for children in the home. Passive-aggressive parents are often thought of as pleasant parents who hide their anger. One of our seminar participants wrote the following:

> My parents never fought or expressed an angry word to each other as long as I can remember. But I knew when they were angry with each other, and I felt sad when they would withdraw and not speak. I remember asking them what was wrong, but they always would answer, politely, "Everything is fine."

Likewise, adults who have been socialized along the second developmental pathway often make parenting statements such as the following:

- "Shame on you for talking to me that way."
- "Don't you know it's a sin to be angry at your parents?"
- "Until you show me the respect I deserve by apologizing, you will stay in your room!"
- "You just wait! You'll be sorry you acted that way, because good girls don't use that language."
- "Show me you're not angry at me anymore. Come give me a hug and a kiss."

These parents believe that they are doing the right and socially appropriate thing by squelching anger in front of their children; the unintended consequence is that they provide their children with no model or instruction for the healthy expression of anger. Children of passive-aggressive parents often learn that expressing anger directly is taboo. In turn, they become the next generation of adults who lack this key skill for establishing intimacy in close relationships.

With this backdrop in mind, let's revisit the five levels of passive-aggressive behavior and take a look at typical patterns of hidden anger in close adult relationships.

Level 1: Temporary Compliance

Marriage and family therapists could write volumes on the many variations of temporary compliance, given how often clients present with complaints at this level. Though the core issues of masked anger that underlie it are far more complex, this most common way of inciting anger in others is often the straw that breaks the family's back.

You Are Invited

Mindy was an extrovert who loved to socialize with family, friends, and neighbors. Her husband, Tom, was introverted. While he could handle the chit-chat of dinner parties and backyard barbeques, if left to his own devices, he would much rather stay home alone. This dynamic in their relationship set them up for an often-repeated scenario: the stalled RSVP.

Mindy would receive an invitation to a party, which she would mention to Tom. Tom would pleasantly ask the date and politely tell Mindy to e-mail it to him at his office so that he could check his calendar, not committing one way or the other. Mindy would convey the date promptly and wait for his answer, so that she could RSVP. She would wait and wait. She would become irritated and e-mail a second time that week. Four or five days later, she would ask in person again, reminding Tom that she needed to give the party host a response. Mindy swore she was not a nag by nature, but this "dance" with Tom brought out her inner pest.

Time and time again, whether they attended the event or not, the end result was the same: The host felt somewhat slighted because of the delayed response to a friendly invitation, Mindy felt irritated at Tom for making her wait so long for a simple yes or no, and Tom felt justified in instructing Mindy not to let the little things in life get her so upset and to go with the flow more often.

Toddlers learn that if they put their hands on a hot stove, they will get burned. Usually, one of these intense experiences is enough to teach them for a lifetime. Not so with adults facing passive aggression! Despite conflict after badly ending conflict, adults in passive-aggressive relationships seem drawn to the flame of the behavior time and again. Members of passive-aggressive couples will comment, "It seems like we're always having the same argument over and over." The issue may change from day to day, but the core problem stays the same.

The Honey-Do List

Jen begins most weekends by leaving a "Honey-Do" list for her husband Ryan. In her mind, the list is filled with simple things—hanging a picture, fixing a leaky faucet, cutting the lawn, and so on. In Ryan's mind, the degree of difficulty is irrelevant. He bristles at what he perceives as Jen's efforts to control him and has learned exactly how to resist her lists. Early in their relationship, Ryan would try to talk his way out of the list with excuses or simply refuse the tasks, but he quickly learned that temporarily complying with her requests was a far more effective—and satisfying—strategy. Once he learned the art of temporary compliance, their weekends passed like clockwork:

1. Jen left list for Ryan (in obvious spot) on Friday night or Saturday morning.

2. Ryan pretended not to see list (temporary blindness).

3. By noon (or so) on Saturday, an already-flustered Jen would hand Ryan the list.

4. Ryan would smile, read it over, and make his own shopping list for the supplies he'd need for her projects.

5. By 4 P.M. on Sunday, Jen would sigh loudly and awkwardly page through Do-It-Yourself manuals, trying to figure out basic plumbing or spackling techniques. When Ryan would pass by on his way to the kitchen, she would explode in anger, unleashing her frustration over a weekend gone by with no progress on the list.

6. Ryan would remain calm as Jen ranted. When she was done, he would calmly say any of the following statements:

   - "I didn't know you wanted it done *this* weekend, honey."

   - "Why didn't you tell me it was so important to you?"

   - "I could have easily gotten to it yesterday if I had known it was so important."

   - "What's the rush?"

   - "I was just on my way to make us a nice dinner. Would you like me to go fix the faucet instead?"

   - "Why are you always so angry about these things?"

Level 2: Intentional Inefficiency

At this level, a spouse or other family member agrees to a request without forgetting, stalling, or delaying but then carries out the task in a way that is purposefully unacceptable or that will be upsetting. The following two examples involve prospective in-laws and a married couple, respectively.

For Whom Does the Wedding Bell Toll?

This is probably the first of many tales to tell about the source of my stress: my mother-in-law. Joni and I had just become engaged. Fantastic! Everything was great until I learned that my future in-laws were planning an engagement party extravaganza with rented hall, catered food, band, the whole bit. Okay, I guess I could live through it. It should be a fun party, anyway.

As time went on, I began feeling that the party was getting out of hand. Every time I made a suggestion about the music or some other component, my idea was politely dismissed as inappropriate. After several weeks, I became all too aware of exactly who was financing this thing and who was deciding on all the arrangements. At some point, I agreed to show up for the party, but that would be the total extent of my participation.

One week before the extravaganza, Joni's mother began dropping hints: "You look so nice without a beard." "Don't you think a trim would make your hair look neater?" "Don't come right away; maybe you and Joni should arrive later, after the guests." That was it! She was making too many suggestions, and I felt she was inhibiting my personal freedom. She even went so far as to buy me a suit for the occasion and suggested I might want to select a shirt and tie.

The Christmas before, Joni had made me a pendant composed of parts from several junked clocks. I decided to wear that to the party. I felt it was totally appropriate and quite a handsome piece. When my future mother-in-law heard about my plans, she broke down into sobs of distress, crying uncontrollably. It did my heart good! But after a moment, the impossible happened! I actually felt sorry for her! I wore a tie, but not the suit, arrived in time to greet the guests, and had a good time. But for that brief moment in time, revenge was sweet!

A Quick Run to the Store

Tom and Mary plan to host a brunch for 20 of Tom's family members. Neither of them wants to host the event, but both feel a family obligation to do so. Mary labors in the kitchen for 2 days preparing the meal. She also single-handedly cleans the house in preparation for the guests. With each task she completes, she feels ever more angry at her husband for not doing anything to contribute to the party for his relatives. Tom, on the other hand, feels increasingly irritated with Mary for scheduling the event on a weekend during which he had planned to play golf with friends.

Two hours before the guests are scheduled to arrive, Mary asks Tom if he will run to the grocery store to pick up a few last-minute items. He readily agrees, liking the idea of a get-out-of-the-house-free pass while also getting credit for being helpful. She hands him the short, five-item list and thanks him for his willingness to make the run. A full hour later, Mary calls Tom on his cell phone, asking if anything is wrong, because he has not yet returned home. He says that he is just fine and is standing in the check-out line. Hearing her exasperation, he adds that the store was crowded. When he finally gets home, Mary grabs the bag and sends Tom upstairs to quickly change his clothes. From the top of the stairs, he can hear her groan as she unpacks the too-small can of evaporated milk and the wrong brand of sauce. Tom knows well that his shopping left her with too little time to bake and not quite enough ingredients to bake with, but he felt justified that she got what she deserved for interfering with his weekend plans.

When the guests arrived, Mary asked Tom to get their drinks. As his relatives stood around with their coats on, Mary barked at Tom to get their coats. He replied calmly, "I was getting their drinks, as you asked me to." Tom's family whispered about Mary "cracking the whip" on Tom, and Tom nodded when his brothers lamented Mary's attitude.

We can't leave out a dishwasher example:

"Where does this go?"

Peter's wife asks him to unload the dishwasher just as he is about to go upstairs for bed. In the morning, she comes downstairs to find the machine completely empty. More than half of its load is neatly stacked along various countertops. When asked about the job, Peter nonchalantly explains that he wasn't sure where the various dishes were supposed to go, so he left them out rather than putting them in the wrong cabinets. His wife finishes the task on her own.

Level 3: Letting a Problem Escalate

In Level 3 passive aggression, hidden anger is characterized by inaction. A Level 3 passive-aggressive act is one that fails to prevent an easily foreseeable problem from occurring or that fails to take action to keep a situation from worsening. The following examples all involve married couples.

Driving Mr. Daisy Crazy

I have been in therapy for the past 2 years to work out a better marital relationship with my husband. Sometimes I wonder why we ever got married in the first place, since we are such different personality types and enjoy such opposite lifestyles. Jerry is a powerful, successful, and super-organized attorney. He believes the early bird gets the worm; he gets up each morning at 5:00 A.M. Before going to bed at 9:30 P.M., he programs the coffeemaker so his coffee will be hot and ready at 5:00. Following coffee, he has a large glass of orange juice and a bowl of Total cereal. He exercises for the next 30 minutes using his weights and treadmill. Then he showers, shaves, and dresses and is off to work by 6:30. Intermittently, I wonder if he is a robot.

What I like to do is to go to bed after watching *Late Night With Conan O'Brien* and get up around 9:30 A.M. to catch the end of *The Today Show*. I consider myself a relaxed, laid-back, easygoing woman who doesn't like to race through life. I enjoy reading the newspaper in the morning, talking to my friends, and participating in various community activities. Our marriage seems to operate on the unexpressed agreement of "I won't bother you if you don't bother me!"

This arrangement works out most of the time, except when we go on one of our weeklong car trips to a national monument or park. I dread these trips and find them anything but pleasant. Jerry, of course, organizes these trips down to the minute. His plan is to have the car packed, gassed, and ready to go the night before we leave. We are to get up at 5:30 A.M. and leave at 6:00 A.M., with a Thermos of coffee in hand. His goal is to drive for 2 hours and then stop for breakfast for 40 minutes. Then we are to drive for 3½ more hours and check into a Holiday Inn by 1:00 P.M. We are to unpack, have lunch, take a swim, and do other relaxing activities.

Last August, I had an opportunity to assert myself during one of these trips. Jerry had planned to drive us to the Blue Ridge Mountains of West Virginia. We left at 6:00 A.M., on schedule, and drove west on U.S. 70. In 1 hour we would turn south on U.S. 81. Jerry was driving faster than the speed limit, although it was a foggy and damp day. His driving was beginning to irritate me, but I bit my lip. Then I noticed a highway sign flash by: "U.S. 81, 1 mile." I realized Jerry didn't see it, since he was not slowing down. I decided not to say anything to him until we'd passed the exit. Two miles later, I said, "Darling, have you changed your mind about turning on U.S. 81?" He looked surprised and said, "Do you mean we missed it?" I nodded and he shouted, "Why didn't you tell me?" "Darling," I replied sweetly, "You are so well organized I never thought for a moment you had made a mistake. I just thought you had decided on a different route." Jerry was beside himself and had to drive another 8 miles before finding the next exit to turn around. His mistake meant his schedule was off by 20 minutes, but I had a day's worth of satisfaction.

"Gee, honey, I'm sorry"

I never thought I was a passive-aggressive person until I attended your seminar. The diagnostic categories were so clear, I had no difficulty identifying myself. I did have a problem admitting I felt some joy and satisfaction when I got back at some frustrating person. The one example I will always remember happened when I was angry with my wife for nagging me. I deliberately got back at her. At the time I felt vindicated, but later I felt guilty.

I have been married to Cynthia for 15 years, and she has several behaviors that irritate me. The one that is most upsetting to me is her obsession to be at work on time, regardless of the driving conditions. Let me explain.

We both work in downtown Chicago, so we drive together, or, more precisely, I need to drive her to her office by 8:30 A.M. Because it is a 45-minute commute, we leave our condo no later than 7:30. This particular Thursday, I had a difficult night sleeping. I was up three times, so when the alarm went off at 6:30, I was not in a good or active mood. Cynthia, of course, woke up in high gear and was finished dressing before I started my shower. Then she started in on me.

"Robert, do you realize you have only 25 minutes before we leave?" "Robert, you need to hurry up." "Robert, you know I have an important meeting this morning, so I can't be late." "Robert, I don't think you will have time for breakfast." "Robert, I am going to be mad if you make me late." "Robert, why do you do this to me? Why can't you get organized in the morning?!" By this time, I was boiling, but I didn't say anything.

We left at 7:50, and before I drove out of the garage, she said, "I know I am going to be late, and it is all your fault! I don't know why I even drive with you in the morning!" I didn't reply, but I thought her last angry comment seemed like a good idea to me. We didn't speak to each other the remainder of the trip, but I remember I deliberately drove in the slowest lane and stopped at every red light possible. We arrived at 8:30. She jumped out of the car, sarcastically said, "Thanks for the ride," and slammed the door. I started to drive away when I noticed she had left her briefcase with all the documents she needed for her meeting on the backseat. I quickly accelerated and smiled, "Okay, Cynthia, now it's your turn." I even had the pleasant thought that her compulsive boss might yell at her and tell her she needed to get better organized in the morning.

When I arrived at work, I called her and said in a sympathetic tone, "Cynthia, I just discovered your briefcase on the backseat of the car and called you immediately." Cynthia said she realized she left it the moment she entered the building, but when she ran back to the curb, I was gone. I told her I was sorry I didn't see it sooner. She asked in a subdued tone if I could possibly bring it over to her work. I said I wished I could, but I had a scheduled appointment all morning. She thanked me for the call and said she would pick it up during her lunch hour. I knew she was close to tears, but when she hung up, I remember saying to myself, "Touché!"

Level 4: Hidden but Conscious Revenge

At Level 4, hidden but conscious anger, the adult acts definitively, but covertly, to get back at a spouse or family member. Revenge at this level brings satisfaction—even joy—to the passive-aggressive adult, despite the genuine and lasting damage it can do to his or her victim. In previous chapters, we have talked about hidden revenge at the level of "lost" keys and slashed tires. Backhanded compliments, unsolicited advice, and unwanted gifts are also classic examples of how adults engage in Level 4 passive aggression. Beneath the veil of "I was only trying to help" lies a very different and crystal-clear message that both the sender and the receiver perceive.

> Backhanded compliments, unsolicited advice, and unwanted gifts are also classic examples of how adults engage in Level 4 passive aggression.

Backhanded compliments come in many forms, but they always take the angle of twisting something evidently positive into a subtly negative jab. The impact of the jab steals the joy and pride from the original compliment:

- "You have done so well for yourself, especially considering that you never even finished high school."

- "I am so impressed with how far you have come! Think about how badly you had messed up your life just a year ago."

- "Your finishing time in the race was amazing! For your age group, you did great!"

- "It's amazing that you know how to parent as well as you do, considering what a terrible family life you grew up with!"

Advice is a wonderful thing when it is requested and when it is given with the receiver's true best interests at heart. Unsolicited advice becomes a kind of backhanded compliment when the receiver is wounded by the words and the advisor's true intentions are to criticize.

How I Met My Future Mother-in-Law

My first encounter with my future mother-in-law showed me a lot about what my marriage would be like. If I had had the skills to recognize passive-aggressive behavior at the time, I might have saved myself years of frustration and heartache.

Ten minutes into our initial meeting, my fiancé's mother advised me about how I could get rid of the "awful redness" that covered my cheeks. By the end of the evening, my posture and career choice had also come under her uninvited advisement. Though she had said nothing wrong that I could put my finger on, I left with the feeling that I could do no right.

As they say, the apple doesn't fall far from the tree. In my marriage, I have come to expect criticism, thinly veiled as advice, on most of the things I do. Whether it be my parenting, my decorating sense, or how I clean the house, nothing I do is good enough to be above the loving guidance of my husband or the indelicate suggestions of his mother.

A person operating at Level 4 picks gifts for others, not based on what the receiver genuinely desires, but rather on a specific passive-aggressive statement that the gift-giver wants to make.

The Gift That Keeps on Giving

From as early as I can remember, I enjoyed being around kids. As an adult, I taught in a special education classroom, earned my EdD, and eventually became a school principal. Although I earned a nice income and loved my career, my wife made it clear that my line of work did not meet her "three-piece suit" standards. In her eyes, true "professionals" wore formal business attire—not the khakis and button-downs that fit my academic environment.

Upon my promotion to principal, she threw a party. With a crowd to witness her spectacle, she asked me to unwrap her gift—a $1,200 three-piece suit. She read the card aloud: "Congratulations on your promotion. This suit will give you confidence to achieve your potential." While my family and friends admired the gift, I quietly fumed. I was deeply wounded by the covert message that I knew my wife was sending. Though our crowd of guests considered my recent promotion to be indicative of my success, my wife's public display conveyed her private belief that I still had a long way to go and needed her help to get there.

In Chapter 6, we saw how students can use the Internet to engage in Level 4 passive-aggressive acts of cyber-bullying. Likewise, adults can use the World Wide Web as their marketplace for hidden but conscious revenge. The free classifieds site www.craigslist.com featured the following classified ad:

"House being demolished. Come and take whatever you want."

The house belonged to a woman whose niece, who was angry with her, placed the ad. The result was almost $20,000 in theft and damages.

Woman's Revenge

"Cash, check, or charge?" I asked, after folding the items the woman wished to purchase. As she fumbled for her wallet, I noticed a remote control for a television set in her purse. "So, do you always carry your TV remote?" I asked. "No," she replied, "but my husband refused to come shopping with me, and I figured this was the most evil thing I could do to him legally."

Level 5: Self-Depreciation

In Level 5, self-depreciation, which is most pathological level of passive aggression, a person is willing to bring real harm to him- or herself in order to also hurt or get back at his or her spouse.

Less for Lester

I was a plump teen in a slim family. I stopped eating normally at about age 15. Rather rapidly I lost so much weight that my parents insisted on therapy, which culminated in my hospitalization for anorexia nervosa. The doctors helped me begin to eat enough to maintain a thin but not skeletal appearance.

When I met Les, my husband, I weighed about 100 pounds and looked fine, though fragile. My husband wanted me to put "more meat on my bones" and sometimes became annoyed when he was eating steak and pasta and I, my salad. Recently, the issue of my gaining 10 pounds became the central topic for continued discussion with Lester. He constantly bugged me to gain the extra weight. When he decided to go visit his parents by himself for a week, I was verbally supportive of his independent activity and understanding of his need for a meeting with his aging folks. Although he questioned me about my feelings, I assured him that I really wanted him to enjoy this time alone with his family.

Upon his return, however, he found me awaiting his arrival weighing 5 pounds less. Instead of dealing with my true feelings related to his private meeting and feelings of exclusion, I acted out in a way that I knew would annoy him. I consider my weight loss a passive-aggressive act.

Both dangerous weight loss and excessive weight gain are ways that passive-aggressive individuals can bring genuine physical harm to themselves as a way of getting back at a family member.

Infidelity

Rebecca is unhappy in her marriage. She persistently argues with her husband about his spending more time at home with the family, yet she covertly pushes him away whenever he abides. After 7 years of marriage, she reveals to her husband that she has been having an affair.

Many feel that adultery is the ultimate betrayal in a marriage. Murphy and Oberlin (2005) wrote that "infidelity is often less about sexual satisfaction and much more a realistic barometer of other emotions, including hidden anger built upon unrealistic expectations, beliefs, or fears" (p. 48). As noted earlier in the chapter, passive aggression interferes with intimacy in a marriage. For a partner who is uncomfortable with true emotional expression, infidelity might be seen as an escape route from the threat of emerging intimacy. The act of having an affair can be a self-depreciating, passive-aggressive one. It blocks the partner from coming any closer and threatening a protected, hidden, inner world of emotion, but at the same time it potentially destroys the marriage and turns the social, emotional, and financial worlds of both partners, any children, and many extended family members upside down.

Summary

Sometimes it is difficult in the fields of education, psychology, and mental health to select examples of an individual's troubling behaviors that most others will recognize and to which they will be able to relate. This is certainly not the case with passive aggression. Rather, our difficulty has been in narrowing down the examples so that we illustrate our concepts without hitting our readers over the head with them. When it comes to hidden anger within close relationships, this is especially true because within the perceived safety and bonds of marriage and family, adults engage in confusing, frustrating compliant defiance with great frequency.

Likewise, in the workplace, where many adults spend most of their waking hours, passive-aggressive acts are quite commonplace. Coming up, we will explain why the office is such an ideal venue for passive aggression and study examples of how the behavior is exhibited by employees and bosses alike.

Passive-Aggressive Behaviors in the Workplace

8

Many workplace cultures share several common components that make them ripe for passive aggression:

1. *People spend a lot of their time there.* Second to the home (where most people spend between 6 and 10 hours of their time, sleeping!), many adults spend more time at work than anyplace else. Whether situational or chronic, passive-aggressive behavior is likely to come out wherever a person spends a great deal of time.

2. *Relationships tend to form wherever a person spends a great deal of time.* Whether in the course of strictly business or over friendly lunches, enduring relationships develop in most workplaces, and within relationships, passive aggression occurs. Unlike depression, anxiety, schizophrenia, or most other psychological syndromes, passive aggression always takes at least two to tango. A passive-aggressive person must have a foe on whom to subtly unleash hidden anger.

3. *The professional atmosphere of most workplaces makes emotional expression unacceptable.* Yet, even in a formal business environment, emotions are aroused over any number of things—workload, work quality, "the big deal," promotions, respect, talent, intelligence, credibility, and other very personal issues that touch upon an individual's self-worth. These heartfelt and personal emotions need an outlet.

4. *The hierarchy of most workplace cultures makes direct expression of anger seem like insubordination.* An employee who feels slighted by her boss does not have the ability, in most workplaces, to tell the boss how she really feels without risking her very career. It is also true that a boss, frustrated by the quality of a supervisee's work, would violate both written and unwritten company policies by giving the employee completely candid feedback. Words in the workplace must be chosen with extreme care, thereby making it an ideal environment for passive aggression.

5. *The hierarchy of a workplace culture may resemble a dysfunctional home environment.* For a child who traveled along a passive-aggressive developmental pathway, in which a parent was all-powerful and the child had no recourse for the direct expression of anger, a hierarchical workplace culture may trigger his template for perceiving authority figures as hostile (see Chapter 2). Regardless of the accuracy of the perception, the passive-aggressive employee will tend to react as if any authority figure in the workplace is the abusive adult from his younger days.

6. *The heavy reliance on electronic communication gives an ideal cover for passive-aggressive exchanges among coworkers.* In a face-to-face or live telephone or video interaction, body language and tone of voice betray anger and hostility. As the saying goes, it's not what you say, it's how you say it. Being able to see and hear people while they are talking is very important to understanding their true message. The use of e-mail and other

electronic communications in many companies has completely altered the way in which businesspeople interact—and the ways in which meaning is transmitted. When big deals, major decisions, and important working relationships are established and maintained without traditional personal contact, efficiency is won, but important messages may be lost—or hidden.

7. The teamwork dynamic encouraged by many workplaces can be a great venue for obstructionism and loss of accountability. The covert actions of one passive-aggressive team member can stop the whole show and sabotage entire projects subtly enough that his responsibility is not readily apparent or can be tenaciously justified.

8. It is often difficult to fire employees. Human resources policies, designed with the best intentions of protecting workers, can make it especially challenging to terminate a passive-aggressive employee. Picture the intentionally inefficient employee who litigiously meets all minimum standards. If confronted, he puts up a good, victim-inspired fight, claiming that the boss just doesn't like him and is harassing his completely acceptable work performance. Picture the disgruntled supervisee who makes it a point to go over her boss' head while the boss is away on a business trip, or the spiteful coworker who "accidentally" demotes a colleague in the cc: line of a memo as a way of publicly slighting her. The passive-aggressive employee is always armed with a plausible explanation for any of these behaviors and is expert in casting himself in the role of victim to his outwardly angry accuser.

By the nature of their covert or "justifiable" acts, passive-aggressive employees are skilled at evading the long arm of workplace law. That's why passive aggression has been termed "the perfect office crime" (Sandberg, 2005). While the passive-aggressive person's behavior impacts the big picture of an organization's productivity and morale, his or her piece-by-piece acts of insubordination and sabotage are often extremely hard to nail down. Let's examine passive-aggressive behaviors in the workplace, level by level.

Level 1: Temporary Compliance

The desire to be recognized for one's contributions and abilities is universal and often fundamental to an employee's productivity in the workplace. For workers who feel underacknowledged and underappreciated, passive-aggressive acts of temporary compliance can be a satisfying way of getting back at those who they believe overlook them.

"I'm too good for that!"

Phil sits in his boss' office, taking ample notes on the objectives of a new assignment. He nods in agreement, shakes his boss' hand, and then quietly places his notepad alongside a waiting-to-be-emptied trash receptacle as he exits the office on his way to his cubicle. Beneath his angry professional smile, Phil seethes at what he perceives as a lowly task of writing a company newsletter. Considering the request beneath him, he plans for how he will evade it. Will it be something he apologetically "forgets" because he was so busy with crafting the department's new marketing plan? Will he "put it on the boss' desk" and be as puzzled as the boss about what happened to it? Or will he be the victim of a hard-drive crash (again!), in which the entire newsletter was lost? Whichever option Phil chooses, two things are certain: He will not explain to his boss how he truly feels, and he will never sink so low as to write that newsletter.

The ability to manage multiple priorities is often high on a hiring supervisor's list of desirable qualities when selecting candidates for employment. For the passive-aggressive employee, resentment over workload often results in neglecting to complete certain tasks and generally doing less after agreeing to do more.

"I can't handle so much!"

Jane was stressed out at work. Her To-Do list was a mile long, and she angrily felt like every time she crossed off one task, her manager added three more. She believed that if she went to her boss and explained that her workload was overwhelming, the boss would remind her, in his patronizing way, that everyone on the team was carrying a heavy load and that Jane had to become better at juggling projects if she wanted professional respect. Jane concluded that admitting her struggles with managing so many different tasks would be tantamount to admitting incompetence, so she decided on a different route. Before important deadlines, Jane used sick days. During meetings, she accidentally left critical files back at her desk. When traveling, her Blackberry would malfunction, leaving her completely disconnected. If there was an excuse for uncompleted work, Jane had it, and if she were confronted about her excuses, each one appeared airtight. Jane's ultimate moment of satisfaction came when her boss referred her to the organization's employee counseling service. Jane verbally complied with his recommendation and watched him squirm as she waited 6 weeks before calling to make the appointment. During the fifth week, her boss accepted a job in a new department.

Jane's scenario is not uncommon; passive-aggressive employees often outlast their coworkers. With forgetfulness, excuses, procrastination, stubbornness, and resistance, they drive away those who try to manage them or accomplish tasks around them. Meanwhile, the passive-aggressive person's enjoyment of work actually increases as this process unfolds—the demands of the job become fewer, and the suffering of coworkers increases. Workplaces become ripe for passive aggression when the behavior is perceived as rewarding.

"I never got the message!"

Joe made the "Oh, I must have just missed you" excuse a professional way of life. His coworkers joked that he had hidden cameras planted around the office and knew exactly when someone had stepped away from his or her desk. He would choose those moments—however brief—to call them and leave a voice message rather than speaking with them face to face. Sometimes he would post a note on their door and dash away, so he would not be there when they returned. Likewise, Joe heavily favored e-mail communication, even when personal contact was easier or necessary to clarify a complex issue.

Though he was big on communicating in these indirect, less personal ways, he was notoriously bad about responding to the same type of message. The partner to his "Oh, I must have just missed you" excuse was his "I never got the e-mail" or his "My voicemail was down all day" response. He had an uncanny knack for walking past Post-it notes on his office door and even seemed oblivious to those taped right to his computer screen. Temporary blindness, deafness, and brain damage all conveniently came and went when it came to responding to his coworkers.

Brevity was the soul of the responses he did get around to making. He would often answer long e-mails that contained multiple issues and questions with single, vague sentences or even yes or no replies that did not specify which question was being addressed. Joe's terse responses frustrated the recipient because of the delay they caused to productivity and the uncertainty they left about his meaning. If a coworker tried to reach Joe by telephone to clarify a message, he inevitably did not answer. If a coworker stopped by his office, he was predictably not there or "just about to leave" for an important meeting.

In addition to infuriating others and delaying productivity, vague replies to electronic communications have a third function for the passive-aggressive employee: They insulate him or her from blame when a project goes awry. An employee can disavow responsibility by claiming, "That's not what I meant" or defend his role by saying, "You misunderstood what I wrote."

As the final example of temporary compliance, it is important to recognize that passive aggression does not always flow from the bottom up in a workplace. Just as parents can behave in passive-aggressive ways toward their children, so some bosses are most certainly capable of taking out their hidden agendas on their supervisees.

The Boss' Recommendation

The director of operations in my company had it out for me. I'm not sure if she was threatened by me or what, but she seemed to enjoy making my professional life as difficult as possible. Three months ago, I let her know that I had tossed my hat in the ring for a promotion. To my face, she congratulated the decision and told me that I was the best qualified candidate for the job. She even said she'd be happy to speak with the department manager on my behalf. What a mistake I made accepting that offer! I'll never know if she actually said anything, but I do know that just prior to the hiring decision, I was working on a high-profile project that she ultimately controlled.

Our company did not have the optimal software for the project, so I went through the purchasing bureaucracy, which ended with her signature. She let the requisition form sit on her desk for weeks! When my boss called her about it, she claimed that she had meant to sign it but that it had just gotten buried under a stack of other papers. She assured him she would process it that day, yet it sat untouched. In the end, I was unable to meet my project deadline because I waited too long for the software. For me, it was a very public professional flop and needless to say, I did not get the promotion for which she had assured me I was a shoe-in.

Level 2: Intentional Inefficiency

For many employees, ego would get in the way of their conducting work in a way that was beneath their abilities. For a passive-aggressive person, however, the drive to act out hidden anger supersedes the desire for recognition of competence. In the following examples, we will look at how passive-aggressive employees and supervisors conduct business in a mindfully unacceptable way.

"This cubicle will never do!"

I was a superstar in an office that didn't have the resources for my talent. For the 15 employees in our department, there were only two offices. The rest of us were assigned to work on top of each other in small, noisy cubicles. I understood that our director had dibs on one of the offices, but I could never accept why I didn't get the other. I needed to be able to close a door and conduct important discussions. Likewise, when the three laptop computers available to us were assigned, I was excluded and was left with an older, slower desktop model. I needed a computer that could handle complicated software and that I could take home with me to carry out my heavy workload after hours. The last straw came when my company cell phone was recalled. My boss explained that the organization felt that cell phones were an unnecessary expense for our department, but I took it as a final stripping of my professional dignity. "If this is how they're going to handle it," I thought, "I'll show them how well I can play the cards I am dealt."

From that day forward, I ceased to amaze with my work, though I was careful not to let my drop in performance seem like my own fault. When I was assigned the task of impressing a potential client, I gleefully suggested a face-to-face meeting in my cubicle. Nothing like giving personal attention to customers, and I wanted to share the great resources my company had to offer by displaying the total lack of privacy and quiet afforded by my cramped cubicle. When I was assigned tight deadlines, I worked and worked for exactly 8 hours at my desk, and then I worked no more. If my tasks were late, I contritely explained that if I had had a laptop, I could have taken the work home with me and met the deadline. When I was late for important meetings, I would confess that without the cell phone, I was unable to phone ahead that an appointment had run long or that traffic was terrible on the expressway.

Each of my excuses was precisely tied to the lack of resources I was given. I became the superstar of victims, and although I never got the office or laptop that I coveted, I did enjoy watching my supervisor's face each time she tried (unsuccessfully) to reprimand me.

"No one ever told me!"

I supervised a princess. Well, Jolie probably wasn't really a princess, but she did (often!) tell me that, in her country, she was a member of a ruling family. She certainly did carry herself around our office as if she were royalty—above criticism and vocal about her job being beneath her. How she found herself in a clerical position or why she chose to work for minimum wage was completely beyond me—but there she was, on the staff I inherited. I specify that I "inherited" Jolie because it is clear that I never would have hired her had the choice been mine. She clearly did not have the skill set or the personality to sit behind a computer all day and efficiently enter data.

I'm the kind of person who believes in making do with what I have, though, so I tried to be as patient as possible while also ensuring that Jolie pulled her weight. I did not want the rest of her teammates to be unfairly burdened. On task after task, however, Jolie never performed up to standards. She used infuriating stock excuses, such as "No one told me" when confronted about incorrect data entry. One time, she used the "I wasn't trained on how to do that" excuse on an important end-of-year report for the CEO. Not only had I trained her myself on how to do the report, but the responsibility for its lateness would have fallen squarely on my shoulders if I had not realized her actions in time. I knew she knew that *I* knew her true intentions . . . and she and I both also knew that she had won that battle.

In the interests of getting that and future reports done, I got myself into a bad pattern of redoing virtually all of her work on a regular basis. I anguished over how to properly confront her poor performance. In my own nondirect way, I used many one-on-one meetings to encourage her "people" skills, hinting that she could better apply her talents in a different capacity within the organization. At one point, I thought I even had her convinced to resign.

When it came time to give out our company's annual pay raises, Jolie surprised me. She asked for a lofty title change to reflect skills and authority that she in no way possessed. She also asked for a 15% pay raise. I would have thought she was simply out of touch with reality, but for a little smile I caught on her face as she slid her written requests across my desk. In a moment of clarity, I realized that she was in this for the long haul and was enjoying every single minute of the pain, stress, and overtime that I was putting in.

"It's not business; it's personal"

Cameron was the go-to person in our school office. No matter what the time was on the clock or how many other tasks he had going on, he always seemed willing to do just a little bit more. It became a bad habit to rely on him because of this openness to take on more—especially in comparison to employees who turned into pumpkins when the final school bell rang.

Lurking under his mask of willingness to take on tasks, however, was a layer of negativity. Though he never spoke to the principal about it, the teachers were well aware of Cameron's discontent. His complaints dominated teacher's lounge conversations and photocopier chats. Although he was vocal in front of his peers, Cameron's discontent showed up in a different way to administrators. His voluminous work was marred by missed details, important omissions, and critical errors. While never a deadline was missed and never a task turned down, Cameron made his point about the jobs he was assigned through the quality of his final product.

If ever a mistake was pointed out by his supervisor, Cameron had a series of excuses that sounded almost memorized . . . as if he repeated them over and over in his head:

- "I don't know why he's upset. I did the job when no one else was willing to do it."

- "He just wants it done his own way."

- "No one can ever meet his standards. He doesn't approve of anything I do."

- "He doesn't like me. This is personal."

In fact, if you listened close enough to the rehearsed quality of his words and Cameron's too-calm tone, you could almost hear him reciting these words to a parent.

In many organizations, the annual performance evaluation or review is an instrument of great power, held solely in a boss' hands. While many authority figures use it to offer feedback and set goals, a passive-aggressive boss may use the review as a tool for withholding important information.

"There's something missing from my annual review"

My boss could be described as "hot and cold." On a good day, he was warm and friendly, offering positive feedback to his staff. On bad days—and you never knew when they'd come—he was cold, distant, and critical of minutiae. He had been with our organization for more than 20 years and was a fixture of middle management. Though I think his days of aspiring for professional advancement were long gone, it seemed to be a priority for him to make sure that no one on his staff exceeded his position. The annual review was the weapon he used to guard his status.

Don't misunderstand me; the reviews he wrote were never bad. I can honestly say that he never wrote an untrue word, nor did he cast anyone's work in a questionably poor light. Rather, his was a crime of omission. As they say, "If it isn't written down, it didn't happen." In the world's most terse documents, my boss completed each review to HR specifications but omitted from the company's written record any mention of an employee's significant annual contributions. In his passive-aggressive way, he publicly and officially shortchanged employee accomplishments and ensured that at promotion time, their files would not be earmarked.

Level 3: Letting a Problem Escalate

Teamwork and communication are paramount to the productivity of many organizations. When a passive-aggressive employee chooses not to pull her weight or to withhold critical information, entire operations can be halted or even shut down. The following examples and anecdotes demonstrate real-world scenarios of Level 3 passive-aggressive behaviors:

- A CFO of a small company knows there is no money left in a bank account. Nonetheless, she allows checks to be written against the account. She watches with satisfaction as her perceived adversary, the CEO, is publicly embarrassed and considered responsible by her team of loyal workers. The CFO finds enjoyment in watching the CEO stress out about bounced paychecks, handle phone calls from angry vendors, and tally up the bank fees for the returned checks.

- An employee accidentally jams the photocopier and leaves the scene without alerting anyone in the office or initiating a call for repair, even though he is aware that a very important last-minute copying job needs to be done that afternoon. When the job is ready, the machine is unusable.

- An administrative assistant places a large supply order after the deadline. The following week, her office runs out of supplies that are critical to completing important jobs.

- A supervisor knows that an employee has not been informed about important updates before a presentation to the board of directors. Intimidated by her competence and "rising star" quality, he allows her to go on with the presentation and appear foolish in front of the decision makers.

- An employee calls in sick the day before a major deadline, knowing that his presence would be critical to his team's success. He takes great pleasure in single-handedly foiling the project and in the resulting public affirmation that without him, the team could not succeed.

You're Only as Good as Your Weakest Link

I supervised a truly capable woman whose arrogance made her unbearable. Since there were no grounds for firing her, I devised a strategy for driving her out. Every time a new project came around, I paired her with Thomas, a rather lazy, not-quite-competent employee who was counting the days until his retirement. During the first 6 months of working side by side on four different intensive projects, the woman came to me several times complaining about Thomas and asking to work alone. Though I feigned sympathy for her plight of carrying the burden of a lesser worker, I never removed Thomas from her side. Rather, I added to her list of responsibilities the task of bringing Thomas up to speed. Eight months into my plan, she came to me again with her resignation. She angrily threw her letter across my desk and told me she'd be leaving our organization to work in a place with more competent people. I tried to hide my smile as she stormed out of my office. Mission accomplished!

Hindsight

I recall a situation when I was student teaching and couldn't stand my supervising teacher. Ms. Sutter was a proper, well-organized, tight-lipped woman with the face of a lemon and the disposition of a bulldog. Every day she criticized me about my teaching methods, particularly about my lack of organizational ability, even in front of the students. When she did, I felt both embarrassed and angry. I wanted to give her a piece of my mind, but I had heard through the grapevine not to express my concerns because she would only become more hostile toward me. By the sixth week, I dreaded having to teach under her critical surveillance. I was about to explode, but couldn't. Then I had a chance to get even.

On Wednesday after school, the principal held a staff meeting, and I was asked to attend. Just before entering the teacher's lounge, Ms. Sutter stopped by the restroom. When she came out, I noticed her skirt was tucked in the top of her underpants, causing her thighs to be exposed. I didn't say anything because I knew she would be embarrassed in front of her colleagues, especially since there were several male teachers in the school. When I saw this I just thought, "Perfect, now she knows how it feels to be embarrassed in front of one's colleagues."

Level 4: Hidden but Conscious Revenge

The majority of passive-aggressive acts in the workplace are specific to the situation and have short-term consequences, albeit irritating and inconvenient. Others, however, particularly at Level 4, lead to real damage of professional reputations, work slowdowns, morale busters, and corporate sabotage. Some of the more prevalent Level 4 workplace misdemeanors involve travel and technology:

- A passive-aggressive supervisor makes it a habit to assign travel around important personal occasions in the life of one particular employee. Over his 30th wedding anniversary and the entire week before his daughter's wedding, the employee was assigned to be out of the country. When the employee was booked for travel over his son's college graduation, he tendered his resignation rather than miss the event.

- An employee secretly erases important files from her coworker's computer. The files are irreplaceable and represent months of the worker's time and intellectual property.

- An administrative assistant perpetually makes one coworker's flight reservations at times that cause him undue stress. Whether early in the morning at an airport far from his home, during rush hour traffic after a booked day at the office, or so close to an appointment at his destination that he would have to scramble to arrive on time, travel is made intentionally unpleasant.

- A supervisor alters a PowerPoint presentation without anyone knowing. When an employee gives an important presentation in front of a committee of board members, she becomes flustered and loses face in front of the important crowd.

Though bullying is often thought of as a childhood and adolescent issue, the phenomenon is very much alive among adults and has a prominent role in the workplace as a tool of the Level 4 passive-aggressive employee. The following examples demonstrate a passive-aggressive style of relational bullying; though no fists fly, professional relationships and workplace morale suffer a painful black eye.

Called Out!

I was in a routine staff meeting, giving an update on the status of a job. Though a coworker and I had experienced some friction while working together on the job, I thought we had resolved our troubles, and it never would have occurred to me to mention them in this public forum. Instead, I cited the objectives we had accomplished and put a positive spin on the remaining challenges.

When it was her turn to speak, she took a different approach. In a woe-is-me voice, she volunteered too much personal information over the impact that the long hours she had dedicated to our shared task was having on her family. Her obvious implication was that her long hours and familial burdens were due to my laziness. What's more, our boss allowed her to do it. Though it seemed clearly inappropriate, it was as if the boss didn't know how to cut her off.

I seethed in anger but held my professional tongue during the meeting. Afterward, when I angrily confronted my coworker about her public disparagement of my contributions, she responded with shock. Her weary voice was gone, replaced with a "don't be silly" tone of voice; she assured me that her intention was never to comment on my work and that no one thought that I was at fault. Her patronizing manner made it all worse. I left the encounter feeling frustrated, defeated, humiliated, and baffled over how the situation had gotten so turned around.

The Double Agent

I was doing work I liked for a boss I resented. I thought she had gotten all the breaks and had been promoted to a position that I deserved. Since her boss liked her and was not about to see things my way, I set my sights on her team of supervisees.

For a year, I was the consummate double agent. At my boss' side whenever she needed me, I asserted myself as her trusted ally and confidante. I kept her well informed about the nonsense taking place in the department—the long lunches that Bob took, the way Sheila always delegated her work to others, and how Liza's personal dramas cut into all of our productivity. Most importantly, I made sure my boss knew that Bob, Sheila, and Liza had been seeking me out for consultation and supervision instead of going to her. My intention was to let my boss know that I was the person that the team considered their boss, even though she had the title. Gradually, I made my jabs more personal, letting my boss know that team members didn't like her and quoting various things they would say (or that I would imply that they said). I would never tell my boss these things straight out or approach them as if they were my agenda. Rather, in a meeting that she called or as we walked together to a destination, I would casually bring up an insult that someone else had made toward her, usually with a phrase such as, "Just so you know . . ." I cast myself as her eyes and ears—her faithful watchdog who was just there to protect her.

Of course, all along I was doing the same with Bob, Sheila, and Liza—feeding their frustrations at the boss not being there for them, offering my own help whenever they needed it, and sowing the seeds of workplace distress wherever I could. It got to the point where both sides had become so estranged from each other that they did virtually all of their communication through me. Ours became a workplace of hurt feelings, bad blood, and mistrust—except that everyone seemed to trust me.

It took less than a year of this tense atmosphere for my boss to resign. And given the leadership role I had taken with Bob, Sheila, and Liza, it was only natural for me to slip right into her vacant position, with no objections from the team. I got the promotion I had deserved all along as well as a loyal team to lead.

Level 5: Self-Depreciation

Because of the increased level of formality of most professional atmospheres, the workplace expression of Level 5, self-depreciation, is somewhat distinct from this level of passive-aggressive behavior in the home or in school. When a child dons piercings all over her body or brings home failing grades, her family will most likely be deeply struck by the behavior and will react quickly. When a person gains or loses excessive amounts of weight or risks personal health in other dramatic ways, family members notice and respond.

In the workplace, however, acts of self-depreciation may not be heeded in the same way or even acknowledged at all. If an employee were to change his appearance as a way to become less professional, it would be grounds for firing him and would not hurt the organization. If a supervisor were to skip work or show up to the office intoxicated, he would risk his own reputation and career long before he would cause any satisfying damage to his company. Level 5 passive aggression, while still the most pathological degree of the behavior, is less effective in a workplace, where business trumps personal. Still, there are some examples that show the extent to which a passive-aggressive employee is willing to go to play out his or her hidden agenda at work.

Who's Minding the Bottom Line?

A CFO does not like the leadership of his agency's new president. He feels personally snubbed at being left out of many crucial decisions. His vengeance is to plunge the whole agency into financial ruin. In the process, he destroys his own professional reputation and high-paying position, while bringing substantial media attention to his handling of the finances. Eventually, the CFO faces criminal charges for his actions.

Credential Review

A small charter school is dependent on its community for support in keeping its fledgling doors open. At an open house, one disgruntled teacher makes a point to reveal to visitors that she falsified her résumé and does not have the proper credentials to teach. She explains that the school is so desperate for teachers that they hired her anyway. Once word gets around, the teacher's background is checked and she is immediately fired. However, the damage to the school's reputation is done. Media attention results in decline in enrollment, and the school closes it doors permanently at the end of the next school year.

Summary

From electronic communication to water-cooler gossip, the workplace has countless channels for passive-aggressive communication. From personal reputations to corporate productivity, acts of hidden anger wreak havoc in the workplace. The passive-aggressive employee typically

- avoids responsibility for tasks;
- does less when asked for more;
- takes longer than others to complete work;
- misses deadlines;
- withholds information;
- goes over a boss' head to make him or her appear incompetent or unresponsive;
- leaves notes or uses e-mail to avoid face-to-face confrontation;
- doesn't respond to notes or e-mails;
- follows a superior's guidelines and then publicly complains that the guidelines are of no value;
- arrives late;
- extends the lunch break;
- uses sick days unnecessarily;
- "forgets" or "misplaces" important documents;
- resists suggestions for change or improvement;
- procrastinates;
- embarrasses coworkers in public settings, such as meetings or during presentations;

- obstructs workplace progress, goals, and productivity;

- has a plausible explanation to justify behavior; and/or

- uses these strategies almost all of the time across most situations, as opposed to just once in a while.

The passive-aggressive employee's coworkers are

- upset that their productivity and plans are foiled by the passive-aggressive person;

- frustrated at having to take up the slack of the passive-aggressive person's in-action;

- irritated by the endless stream of excuses that the passive-aggressive person uses;

- confounded as to why the passive-aggressive person gets away with so much; and/or

- angry, while the passive-aggressive person seems perfectly content.

The organization that employs the passive-aggressive employee suffers

- decreased productivity,

- damaged morale,

- increased turnover of valued employees, and

- embarrassing public setbacks.

Up Next

Thus far we have explored the history and true meaning of passive aggression, along with its developmental roots and typical reasons for being used. We've examined five distinct levels of passive-aggressive behavior and shown you how each one is played out in the home, at school, in close relationships, and in the workplace.

We turn now to the third part of this text—what we term the New Psychology of Passive Aggression. The concept of counter–passive aggression will be described, along with the Passive-Aggressive Conflict Cycle, which is a model both for understanding the dynamics of passive aggression and for putting a stop to the exasperating behavior before relationships suffer irreparable damage. Most significant, the process of Benign Confrontation will be taught. This is our step-by-step process for unmasking a person's hidden anger and detoxifying his or her interpersonal style.

Changing Passive-Aggressive Behaviors

Counter–Passive Aggression

In the preceding chapters, the passive-aggressive individual has been our main focus, and the etiology of passive aggression, the dynamics of hidden anger, and the various ways a passive-aggressive person successfully frustrates others at home, at school, in close adult relationships, and in the workplace were discussed. This chapter focuses on a neglected but significant dynamic of passive aggression: the *target* of the hidden anger.

Passive aggression is not a one-person game but rather a match that is necessarily played out against an adversary. In every passive-aggressive dynamic, there is a Player B—the parent, teacher, spouse, coworker, or other foe who inadvertently reinforces the passive aggression. Once a circular pattern of passive-aggressive and counter–passive-aggressive behavior occurs, Player B loses the ability to engage in an enjoyable or comfortable relationship with the passive-aggressive individual, Player A. Player B's choice is either to continue to relate to the passive-aggressive opponent on an emotional roller coaster of confusion, anger, and guilt or to learn to understand and control his or her own counter–passive-aggressive behavior.

The Concept of Counter–Passive Aggression

The concept of counter–passive aggression represents a new insight into the dynamics of passive-aggressive behavior. It has been the missing piece of the psychological puzzle in understanding passive aggression. Counter–passive aggression explains why reasonable and rational persons react to passive-aggressive behavior in irrational, conflict-fueling ways.

To reinforce this concept, consider the relationship between a movie director and his lead actor. The movie director (the passive-aggressive person) tells the actor (the non–passive-aggressive person) that he needs to develop more authenticity in his character. The director demonstrates

> In a stressful situation, a person who behaves passive aggressively will create feelings of anger in a targeted adult. If the adult is unaware of this process, he will act on the feelings of anger and mirror the passive aggression, thus behaving in counter–passive-aggressive ways.

the scene and says, "Now, I want you to mirror my emotions and behavior. I want you to act in this scene exactly like I do. This will not be easy, because you have to give up your normal way of relating to others in order to take on my persona."

This description is exactly what happens when a passive-aggressive person relates to the target of his or her hidden anger (for simplicity's sake, we'll use the generic term "adult" when we refer to the target of the anger). Over time, the adult ends up behaving like the passive-aggressive person, in ways that are not characteristic of the adult's personality. Many times, the adult is shocked and appalled to find him- or herself behaving counter–passive aggressively and dismayed to have acted in such a childish and unprofessional way.

Examples of Counter–Passive Aggression

The following examples illustrate how adults who are not typically passive aggressive react to passive-aggressive behaviors by mirroring them. In all of the examples, the adult fails to confront the passive-aggressive individual about his or her underlying anger. Rather, the adult reacts by behaving in counter–passive-aggressive ways.

In addition to the five levels of passive-aggressive behavior, we have documented four types of counter–passive-aggressive behavior.

Type 1: Counter–Temporary Compliance

This first type of counter–passive aggression is the mirror of temporary compliance. Like the passive-aggressive individual, the targeted adult gets revenge by engaging in behaviors such as procrastinating or feigning temporary blindness, deafness, or brain damage.

Holding on

My 13-year-old daughter usually responds to any request with the comment, "Hold o-o-o-n." Over time, it began to upset me. Last week, she was in a rush to get to a skating party and I was the driver. So I calmly said, "Hold o-o-o-n," and took my sweet time getting ready to go.

The Silent Treatment

I witnessed a counter–passive-aggressive dynamic between my mother and my 3-year-old son, Aidan. At the time, I thought it was simply the most incredible display of immaturity I had ever seen in a grandparent; now I understand it in a different light. Aidan was about to begin his first-ever season of soccer, but his team-issued uniform was miles too big. My mother volunteered to sew it for a better fit. She worked hard at the task, and when she was almost done, she called for Aidan to try it on. Aidan didn't answer her first two calls and met the third one with "Coming, Nana!" She waited, but he didn't come. After 10 minutes, I went to retrieve him. He argued with me about wanting to play trains while I reasoned that trying on the uniform would just take a minute. Aidan reluctantly agreed.

When Nana tried to put the jersey over Aidan's head, he wiggled around to make the job difficult. He kept his arms stiff so that she couldn't get them in the sleeves. He refused to remove his jeans, so she had to try on his shorts over his pants. All in all, Aidan acted like a 3-year-old who wanted to play trains and who didn't want to be interrupted to try on clothing. It was not his best behavior, but it was not entirely surprising, given his stage of development. It was my mother's behavior that won the award for being age inappropriate.

For the rest of her visit with us, she gave Aidan the silent treatment. No matter what he said and no matter what he did, she acted like he was not there. Aidan had never been the recipient of this type of behavior before and thought, at first, that Nana had actually gone deaf. He repeated his words to her at a louder and louder decibel. He got right up in her face to try to gain some acknowledgment. Finally, he sobbed, asking me what was wrong with Nana. Only on her way out the door to go home did Nana pat Aidan on the head and say, "Next time, you'll answer me when I call you."

"I'll bring it tomorrow"

There are a number of passive-aggressive students in my class whom I find irritating, and I didn't realize how they were getting me to reflect their behavior. As I thought about it, I came up with the following examples. Steven would raise his hand, and I would say, "I'll be there in a minute," but I'd never return. Cathy would ask me to bring in the science journal I mentioned, and I would reply, "I forgot. I'm sorry. I'll bring it tomorrow." But I didn't.

Under My Skin

Often, when I ask my husband to do something around the house, he mumbles his answer. I have to ask him to repeat what he said. I know that ordinarily he speaks perfectly clearly. Just this morning, when he asked me to do a favor for him, I purposely mumbled my response. He had to ask, "What did you say?" It now dawns on me that I acted just like my husband.

Type 2: Counter–Intentional Inefficiency

Type 2 counter–passive aggression mirrors the behavior of intentional inefficiency. The adult gets back at the passive-aggressive person by not maintaining customary standards.

Team Colors

Martha has been trying to get her teenage children to take more responsibility for their own household needs, such as doing their laundry. It has been a bit of a battle, because each child resists taking on chores. When her son, Jake, asks her if she can wash his football jersey just 2 hours before a game, Martha agrees. She adds his red jersey to her own load of laundry and tells him it should be ready in an hour. When Jake retrieves his game jersey from the dryer, he finds it has faded to a pale shade of pink! He has no choice but to wear it to the game.

How She Won the Battle but Lost the War

My job is to meet with principals who request special transportation for their students. When I arrived at one school, the secretary told me to go right in. When I entered, the principal was sitting at her desk. I said, "Hello." She didn't look up or reply, but she continued to look through a directory while she kept me standing. After 2 minutes, she said, "What can I do for you?" I wanted to say, "Lady, you can show me some good manners," but I didn't. I explained why I was there and asked her to complete a form justifying her request for class trips.

As she filled out the form, I was still brooding about how rudely she had treated me. When she handed me the forms, I looked at them, thanked her, and smiled. I noticed she had not answered one of the important questions on the form, and I knew her request would be rejected. She would have to reapply and begin at the bottom of the list of requests. I made it clear to my supervisor that the problem was her mistake and not mine.

Several days later, I thought about this situation and I was not happy with the way I handled it. This was not typical of me. I let my feelings get the best of me, but at the time it felt like the right thing to do.

Baby Bag

Whenever I ask my husband for help getting our small children ready for school in the morning, he acts as if he is completely bewildered by the task. Suddenly, a grown man thinks shorts are appropriate for snowy weather and marshmallows are a logical choice for breakfast. Last week, when he asked me to pack a bag for his trip to the movies with the kids, I returned his non-favor. Missing pacifiers, the wrong flavor of juice, and veggie sticks instead of gummy bears answered his request. I thought he could benefit from understanding firsthand the drama of improper kid gear!

Type 3: Intentional Overefficiency

Intentional overefficiency is the opposite of intentional inefficiency. Here, standards are upheld to the extreme. Most adults possess authority and responsibility for carrying out certain policies, rules, and regulations in their homes, at school, or in the workplace. Counter–passive-aggressive adults tend to rely on official standards in an extreme way. They express their anger toward a passive-aggressive individual by hiding behind the letter of the law. They use the rules in counter–passive-aggressive ways that allow them to punish and seek revenge without feeling guilty.

Parents, teachers, and bosses are in ideal positions to effectively employ counter–passive-aggressive strategies because they have the power. Parents can punish their kids and take away privileges. Teachers can call on students, question them, and grade their work. Bosses delegate work and evaluate a supervisee's performance and professionalism. Counter–passive-aggressive adults can justify their behavior by saying, "I was only doing my job."

For example, one of the most effective ways a teacher can get back at a passive-aggressive student is to evaluate his or her work critically. When the student turns in an assignment, the teacher can get out the red pencil and critique it (e.g., *it's too long, it's too short, too fragmented, too many dangling participles, incorrect margins, the i's aren't dotted, the t's aren't crossed, Grade D*).

If the parents confront the teacher by saying their son seems to get an unusual number of red marks on his papers, the teacher can quietly hide behind her professional role and say,

> "Are you criticizing me because I have high standards and took the extra time to give your son realistic feedback? I'm appalled, because most parents complain that teachers don't do enough for their children."

These comments create a perfect Catch-22 situation for the parents while protecting the teacher from further criticism for the student's low grade. The following examples further illustrate how this type of counter–passive aggression is employed.

Searching for the Flaw

I observed this example of a teacher's counter–passive-aggressive behavior during a math lesson. The teacher asked two students to go to the blackboard and answer different problems. Jennifer was given the fraction $8/64$ and asked to reduce it to its lowest common denominator. Jennifer wrote $1/8$ and was praised for her answer. Steve, a passive-aggressive student, was given the fraction $3/285$ and asked to reduce it to its lowest common denominator. Steve thought about it and wrote $1/95$.

TEACHER: Are you sure?

STEVE: (*Quizzical*) Yes, $1/95$.

TEACHER: Are you absolutely sure?

STEVE: (*Confused*) Well, $1/96$?

TEACHER: Well, what is it? Is it $1/96$ or $1/95$?

STEVE: I thought it was $1/95$.

TEACHER: Don't tell me what you think. Tell me what you know. Is it $1/95$ or $1/96$?

STEVE: (*In a state of anxiety*) It's $1/95$.

TEACHER: Certainly it's $1/95$, but look how you wrote your 5!

> She walked over to the blackboard, erased his 5 and made a perfect 5.

TEACHER: You need to write your letters more clearly, or someday it will get you into trouble.

The teacher was successful in frustrating the student by becoming counter–passive aggressive.

Two Can Play This Game

Clarisse, a student with a learning disability who is in my class, had been annoying me for weeks. Last week during social studies, I asked the class, "Who can tell me the complete name of the First Lady?" Clarisse knew the answer and was the first student to raise her hand. I looked at her but called on Don. Clarisse looked disappointed that I didn't call on her. If someone had observed this interaction and asked me why I didn't call on Clarisse, I would have said, "I have 30 students in my class, and I can't always call on her."

Later, I asked a difficult question, "Who can tell me the First Lady's major in college? It was mentioned in your reading assignment last night." It was unlikely Clarisse knew the answer, so I called on her. She began to mumble, stutter, and hem and haw. I said politely, "Clarisse, we want you to be part of this class, but you're really going to have to study more. So, please, please read your assignments." While Clarisse looked embarrassed, I was enjoying the situation and thinking, "This time it was *my* turn."

Too Hurt to Work

Ian was a passive-aggressive employee who thwarted the spirit of his office's policies for years. He was expert, however, at conforming to the minimum letter of all laws, so as never to be successfully disciplined by his supervisor. That is, until he suffered an injury that he could not control. When Ian hurt his back in a skiing accident, he became unable to perform several of the routine duties of his position. Still, there were many tasks he could accomplish, so he assumed he could continue his full-time work. His boss, on the other hand, saw the opportunity he had been waiting for. Borrowing a page from Ian's playbook, he cited the letter of human resources policy as grounds for dismissing Ian from his employment. Though Ian had demonstrated that he could still accomplish 85% of his tasks, the other 15% were enough for his boss to prove to him that two could succeed at the game of upholding minimum policy standards.

Type 4: Counter-Escalation

Counter-escalation is a common response by parents who have passive-aggressive children, particularly if they have a disability. Parents can become so overwhelmed by the constant barrage of passive-aggressive behaviors that they, at times, will allow the child's behavior to escalate. A distinction needs to be made between parents who let the behavior escalate so that the child learns from his or her inappropriate behavior and parents who enjoy their child's subsequent plight. When a parent goes through the pain and decides to let the child experience the logical consequences of the inappropriate behavior, hopefully the child will learn from the experience. This is an appropriate child-rearing technique; however, if the parent is angry with the child's passive-aggressive behavior and enjoys the child's dilemma, the child will not learn anything productive about his or her behavior from the experience. Rather, the child will perceive it as an act of punishment by the parents and not a natural function of his or her own behavior.

Morning Madness

6:30 A.M.
Ugh! I stumble out of bed to awaken my two boys to get ready for school at 7:30. Lewis, who is 8 years old, immediately gets up and goes to the bathroom to brush his teeth, thus commencing his organized pattern of preparing for school. "How easy Lewis is," I mumble as I approach to awaken James, who is chronologically 10 years old but who has the abilities of a 3-year-old when it comes to getting it together in

the morning. His response to my wake-up call is, "I'm tired. I still want to sleep." Unhappy at what appears to be the beginning of yet another unpleasant morning ritual, I leave the room, thinking he can stay in bed, even though he explicitly stated last night it was important for him to get up on time due to unfinished homework and unwashed hair.

7:15 A.M.
Lewis is finishing his breakfast as James, in jeans and shirt but no shoes or socks, enters the kitchen and sits down to eat. While he is eating breakfast, I comment on how little time James has to finish his homework. James starts to panic, realizing that finishing breakfast, finding his shoes, doing his homework, and washing his hair are impossible to accomplish in 15 minutes.

7:30 A.M.
James, after spending a very harried 15 minutes, is ready to leave. As he is going out the front door, I suggest he look at himself in the mirror. He sees that he has not even brushed his hair, let alone washed it. Now he begins to fall apart. "How can I go to school looking like this? Where is a brush?" he asks me. I respond, "Wherever you left it." "Mom, please help me," he pleads. As I go to find the brush, I ask him, "Why can't you ever get ready in time?"

7:33 A.M.
James frantically brushes his hair. As he leaves in an anxious state, I tell him, "Have a nice day, honey," knowing that he will have to run two blocks to catch the bus.

"You should have taken your turn"

I teach in a small elementary school with 16 staff members. Rarely do we have time for a civilized lunch. We usually bring a brown-bag lunch or some dish to warm in the microwave. No one ever seemed to be in charge of the teachers' room. I like my room to be neat and clean, but this room was always a mess by the end of each day.

Three months ago, I suggested we keep a daily cleanup list and take turns being responsible for tidying the area at lunch and at the end of the school day. This seemed to work well for everyone but Mary Anne, who always had an excuse for not tidying up on her day. By the third time she neglected her responsibility, I was really ticked.

The next day, I opened the fridge and saw a little bag marked "M.A." Impulsively, I grabbed her bag, looked around, threw it in the trash can, covered it with other garbage, and hastily left. When she began asking about her lunch, I smiled my secret smile and said nothing. I know this was not the right thing to do. I felt guilty, but I also told myself she deserved it!

Unsaid

The coffee station at our office was headquarters for casual conversation, water-cooler gossip, and passive-aggressive exchanges. When one employee left an anonymous, small yellow sticky note asking others to keep the area clean, a war of unspoken words began. The next day, a bigger yellow note covered the original note with sarcastic words about office cleanliness. The conflict escalated as the week went on; bigger notes in brighter colors, biting words, even personal insults—yet never a cross word was exchanged face to face. The best illustration of how passive aggressive our workplace had become was when the president of the company got involved, leaving his own note instructing employees to stop writing notes and get back to work.

The Silent Treatment

A man and his wife were having some problems at home and were giving each other the silent treatment. Suddenly, the man realized that the next day he would need his wife to wake him at 5:00 A.M. for an early morning business flight. Not wanting to be the first to break the silence (and *lose*), he wrote on a piece of paper, "Please wake me at 5:00 A.M." He left it where he knew she would find it. The next morning, the man woke up, only to discover it was 9:00 A.M. and he had missed his flight. Furious, he was about to go and see why his wife hadn't wakened him, when he noticed a piece of paper by the bed. The paper said, "It is 5:00 A.M. Wake up."

Summary

Counter–passive aggression occurs when adults mirror the passive-aggressive behaviors of an individual with whom they are interacting. Though this is not the adults' customary pattern of response, they get caught in a circular and lasting cycle of passive-aggressive conflict. In the end, these adults are often bewildered at how the conflict escalated so quickly and surprised at their own troublesome behavior. We have defined four types of counter–passive-aggressive responses:

Type 1: Counter–Temporary Compliance. A person mirrors passive-aggressive behaviors such as feigned forgetfulness, procrastination, or temporary blindness in order to give a passive-aggressive person a "taste of his own medicine."

Type 2: Counter–Intentional Inefficiency. A person purposefully fails to meet or maintain customary standards as a way of getting revenge for passive-aggressive acts that were first directed at her.

Type 3: Intentional Overefficiency. A person uses the extreme letter of the law to justify counter–passive-aggressive paybacks.

Type 4: Counter-Escalation. A person allows a problem to occur or intensify. While the person could easily intervene to stop the problem or improve the situation, she chooses not to, guided by her satisfaction in watching the passive-aggressive person suffer.

A Word of Warning Regarding the Concept of Counter–Passive Aggression

The concept of counter–passive aggression is critical to understanding the psychology of passive aggression. After one of our seminars, a teacher came up to us and said, "I want you to know how much I enjoyed the concept of staff counter–

passive-aggressive behavior. I thought your examples were excellent ways of getting back at students for passive-aggressive behavior. I wondered if you had any other examples I could use in my classroom."

We were stunned and surprised by his comment and said, "I'm afraid we didn't make ourselves clear. We are *not* advocating the use of counter–passive-aggressive behaviors with students. We are trying to do just the opposite. We believe counter–passive-aggressive techniques are *not* to be used in the classroom or at home. We were merely trying to make teachers aware of them, so they won't unknowingly use them."

He looked chagrined, said, "Oh," and walked away. After this incident, we decided to clarify the inappropriate use of counter–passive-aggressive behavior by adults. This incident also illustrates that nothing in life is so simple or so concrete that it cannot be misinterpreted by someone.

The Passive-Aggressive Conflict Cycle

10

As we listened to parents and professionals recount their reactions to passive-aggressive behavior, we were struck by the fact that these intelligent adults were usually unaware of the drip-by-drip hidden and coded message of anger behind the passive aggression. When asked to describe their feelings toward a person with passive-aggressive behavior, the participants consistently described having multiple and confusing feelings. Although they initially found the person to be pleasant and likable, over time their reaction changed first to general irritation and eventually to near rage. Many likened their relationship with the person to riding on a perpetual emotional roller coaster—one week pleasant, the next intolerable.

These educated, seemingly reasonable parents and professionals described becoming emotionally upset by passive-aggressive behavior and admitted to yelling at a passive-aggressive person over minor issues. After such an outburst, they recounted feeling guilty and confused by their unusual flood of emotion. As one participant said,

> "I am a calm and level-headed woman except when I spend any extended time with my sister who is passive aggressive. Then I end up having temper tantrums and feeling guilty about them. What is confusing to me is that I don't have this emotional reaction in my other relationships."

This is not an uncommon description of what it is like to relate to a person with passive-aggressive behavior. The majority of parents, teachers, spouses, and coworkers involved in daily interactions with passive-aggressive individuals are ultimately beaten down by the relationship. Most end up feeling confused, angry, guilty, and doubtful about the stability of their own mental health.

How is it possible for this destructive interpersonal pattern to occur with reasonable adults? How does it happen that the targeted adults end up accepting the blame and responsibility for this dysfunctional dynamic? The answer is clear and painful: They are unaware of the psychology of passive aggression. In the heat

> In the heat of the relationship, even the most intelligent adults can be oblivious to the anger that underlies passive-aggressive behavior and the effect the hidden anger has on their own feelings and behaviors.

of the relationship, they are oblivious to both the anger that underlies passive-aggressive behavior and the effect that the hidden anger has on their own feelings and behaviors.

This chapter connects concepts from the previous chapters into a mosaic, creating a picture of our new psychology of passive aggression. In the early 1960s, we developed the Conflict Cycle Paradigm (N. J. Long & Newman, 1961) to describe the circular and escalating behavior between student and teacher. For years, researchers had studied how an adult's negative behavior can alter and shape a child's behavior; the reverse situation was underexamined. In fact, children and adults alike are capable of shaping each other's behavior, particularly by initiating circular, repetitive, and endless cycles of conflict. The concept is best expressed by the following psychological principle:

> A person in stress can create in others his or her feelings, and if the others are unaware of this psychological process, they will mirror the person's inappropriate behavior.

Overview of the Conflict Cycle Paradigm

The Conflict Cycle Paradigm, which was originally developed to explore student–teacher interactions, can be broadened to include coworkers and spouses. It is a conceptual model that explains the escalating interactions between a person in stress and a nonstressed person. This model, presented in Figure 10.1, consists of five sequential circular stages:

Stage 1: The person's self-concept and irrational beliefs

Stage 2: A stressful event for the person

Stage 3: The feelings of the person

Stage 4: The behavior of the person

Stage 5: The negative reaction by others, which spawns the next cycle of conflict

The predictable sequence of the Conflict Cycle Paradigm is as follows:

1. An incident occurs (i.e., frustration, failure, disappointment) that is processed by the person's self-concept. This process may activate the person's irrational beliefs (i.e., "Nothing good ever happens to me!" "Adults are always demanding!"), which define the incident for the person as stressful.

2. The person's negative thoughts (and not the incident itself) trigger his or her feelings.

3. The person's intense feelings drive his or her inappropriate behaviors.

4. The person's inappropriate behaviors (yelling, threatening, sarcasm, refusing to speak, etc.) incite the person at whom the behaviors are directed.

5. The targeted person picks up on the stressed person's feelings and frequently mirrors the same or similar behaviors (yelling back, threatening, sarcasm, refusing to speak, etc.). These mirrored reactions create more psychological

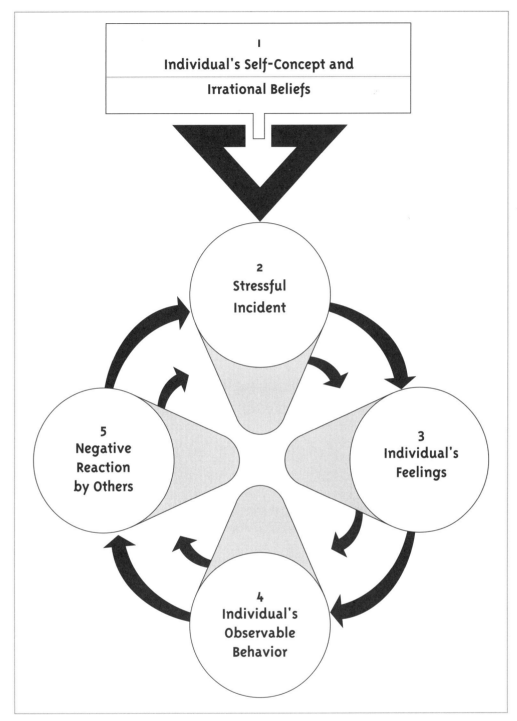

Figure 10.1. The conflict cycle. *Note.* Adapted from "The Conflict Cycle Paradigm: How Troubled Students Get Teachers Out of Control" (p. 327), by N. J. Long, in N. J. Long, W. C. Morse, F. A. Fecser, and R. G. Newman (Eds.), *Conflict in the Classroom*, 2007, Austin, TX: PRO-ED. Copyright 2007 by PRO-ED. Adapted with permission.

stress, new intense feelings, the next round of inappropriate behaviors, and additional rejecting and primitive reactions.

It doesn't take long before the initial manageable conflict escalates into a no-win power struggle.

The Conflict Cycle Paradigm has been used for decades in our Life Space Crisis Intervention trainings to shed light on the dynamics of escalating power struggles. Both youth in crisis and the adults who reach out to them benefit from understanding the predictable process of conflict and recognizing the proper and effective intervention opportunities. In this chapter and the two that follow, you will learn how to use the Passive-Aggressive Conflict Cycle as a tool for understanding and managing passive-aggressive behavior.

The Passive-Aggressive Conflict Cycle Paradigm

When the Conflict Cycle Paradigm is applied to passive-aggressive behavior, our psychology of the angry smile becomes more comprehensive. The Passive-Aggressive Conflict Cycle (see Figure 10.2) is the paradigm for explaining the dynamics of passive aggression.

Stage 1: The Self-Concept and Irrational Beliefs of the Passive-Aggressive Person

Stage 1 represents the person's developmental life history and how the person developed a passive-aggressive personality (see Chapter 2). Passive-aggressive individuals believe that the direct expression of anger is dangerous and destructive and needs to be avoided. For them, the expression of anger is not a misdemeanor but rather a felony. Their psychological solution to this problem is to conceal their anger behind a façade of irritating passive-aggressive behaviors. As with the tip of an iceberg, the real size and power of their anger is out of sight to others.

The following statements were expressed by passive-aggressive students who told us how they feel about anger and passive-aggressive behavior:

- "Angry feelings are upsetting. When people become angry, they yell and scream, and they scare me."

- "When people get angry, terrible things can happen, so there is no telling what I would do if I ever got angry and got out of control."

- "I don't let people know when I'm angry. If they knew what I was thinking, they would hate me and maybe want to kill me."

- "Thinking about anger is wrong, but at times it does excite me."

- "When I'm treated unfairly by others, I'm smart enough to know how to get back at them so they will suffer like they made me suffer."

- "Most teachers and adults are fools. When I'm angry, I can pretend not to hear them."

- "I have to be careful not to let my anger out. It is a demon I have to guard all the time."

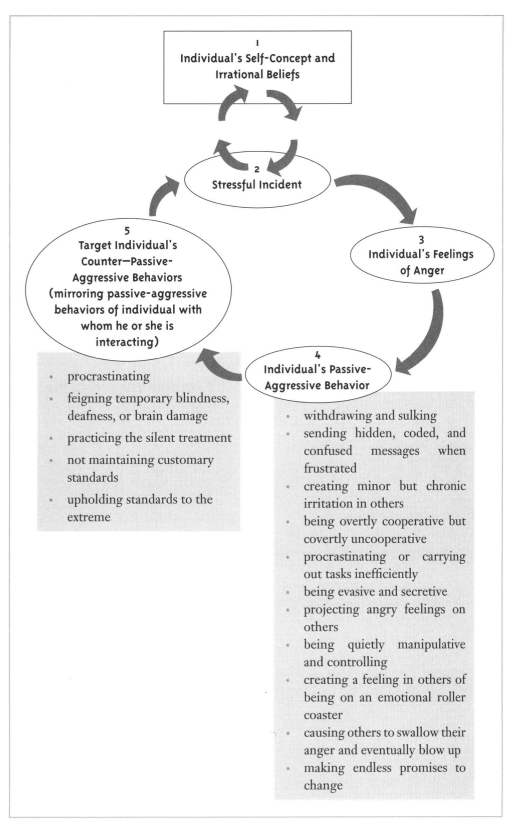

Figure 10.2. The Passive-Aggressive Conflict Cycle. *Note.* Adapted from "The Conflict Cycle Paradigm: How Troubled Students Get Teachers Out of Control" (p. 327), by N. J. Long, in N. J. Long, W. C. Morse, F. A. Fecser, and R. G. Newman (Eds.), *Conflict in the Classroom*, 2007, Austin, TX: PRO-ED. Copyright 2007 by PRO-ED. Adapted with permission.

These personal statements about anger and aggression highlight the intensity of the internalized beliefs held by the students. Once they have established a passive-aggressive way of life, individuals will reinforce their irrational beliefs by responding to new and demanding interpersonal relationships in passive-aggressive ways. They will engage un-suspecting, undeserving others in passive-aggressive conflict cycles that elicit their predictable anger and reinforce their belief systems.

In addition to reinforcing internalized belief systems, secondary rewards for using passive-aggressive behaviors include the following, which

- serve as a defense mechanism and protection from painful feelings of anxiety and helplessness;

- bring order to an unstable world, making relationships predictable and manageable; and

- allow a person to disavow responsibility for personal behavior by blaming others for troublesome, angry interactions.

> Once a passive-aggressive way of life is established, an individual will reinforce her irrational beliefs by responding to new and demanding interpersonal relationships in passive-aggressive ways. The individual will engage unsuspecting, undeserving others in passive-aggressive conflict cycles that elicit their predictable anger and reinforce the passive-aggressive's belief systems.

It is important to note that people with a passive-aggressive personality rarely see themselves as the source of the problem. Moreover, they are proud of their abilities to control anger and to remain rational and calm during confrontational situations. Simultaneously, devising various ways to get back at others indirectly and without their knowledge makes passive-aggressive people feel smart and clever and thus gives them an emotional high and a feeling of power and pleasure at manipulating others so easily.

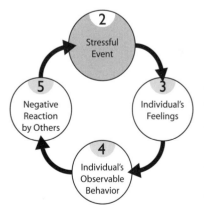

Stage 2: The Passive-Aggressive Person's Stressful Event

The majority of stressful incidents are determined by how a person thinks about them rather than by the reality of the situation. The image of a glass of water that is half full or half empty is an apt metaphor here. It is how an individual thinks about the presenting incident that determines whether or not it is perceived as stressful.

For example, when a person is asked or told to do a specific task, such as helping with a family chore, rewriting a school assignment, doing yard work, or attending a weekend work conference, the task may activate his or her irrational beliefs:

- "I always have to do what they want."

- "I never get to do what I want."

- "They are trying to control me again."

- "They are putting too much pressure on me."

- "These demands are stupid."

Although many people with the same or a similar set of irrational beliefs would immediately express anger or react with aggression in response to what they perceive as an intolerable request, passive-aggressive people reserve their anger for the moment. They push their emotions below the surface for the time being, guided by a more powerful set of irrational beliefs about the nonacceptability of anger. Whether anger over a request surfaces immediately

> A passive-aggressive person pushes his emotions below the surface, guided by a powerful set of irrational beliefs about the nonacceptability of anger.

or whether it is held inside, the same psychological process holds true: Once a connection is made between a presenting event and a person's irrational beliefs, the person will perceive the situation as being stressful.

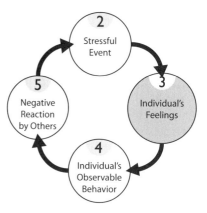

Stage 3: The Passive-Aggressive Person's Feelings

David Burns (1991), a cognitive therapist, wrote, "You feel the way you think" (p. 28). The source of feelings begins in the thoughts and not with the presenting incident or event. It is how a person thinks about an external event, and not the event itself, that triggers the feelings. Positive thoughts about an event (e.g., "I can handle this") trigger positive feelings, whereas negative thoughts (e.g., "Nothing ever works out for me") trigger negative feelings. There are three ways of expressing personal feelings:

1. to act them out ("When I'm angry, I threaten others")

2. to defend against them ("Angry feelings are unacceptable, so I will mask my feelings")

3. to accept them ("Anger is a natural part of my life. It's okay to feel angry when someone is abusive to me")

Of these three choices, the passive-aggressive person has learned to *defend* against his or her angry feelings by using the defense mechanisms of denial, projection, and rationalization. Because the normal feelings of anger, hatred, and rage are unacceptable to the person, they cannot be acknowledged openly. Instead, they are masked and expressed in passive-aggressive ways.

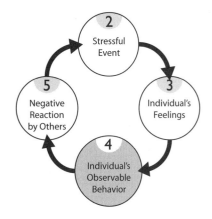

Stage 4: The Passive-Aggressive Person's Behavior

Personal behavior can be expressed in three ways:

1. as an automatic response ("Damn, I caught my finger in the door")

2. as a learned response ("I must not show my anger")

3. as a personal choice ("I decided to ignore his comment")

When we began our study of passive aggression, we thought most passive-aggressive behaviors were due to unconscious forces. After conferring with children and adults who are passive aggressive, we were surprised to find their behavior to be much more a learned response and conscious personal choice. In fact, we were struck by how deliberate many of their acts of passive aggression were. They knew what they were doing and enjoyed the effect it had on others. They were guarded but knew how their passive-aggressive behaviors confused and irritated others. These learned and intentionally chosen passive-aggressive behaviors are very often successful in inviting counter–passive-aggressive feelings in most adults.

> Passive-aggressive behavior is both a learned response and a personal choice; the individual is typically insightful about how her behavior confuses and frustrates others and takes pleasure in observing the impact of her actions.

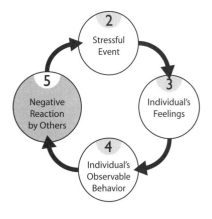

Stage 5: The Negative Reactions of Others

In Chapter 9, the concept of counter–passive aggression was discussed, based on the following psychological principle:

In a stressful situation, the person who behaves passive aggressively will create feelings of anger in a targeted adult. If the targeted person is unaware of this process and acts on the feelings of anger, he or she will mirror the passive aggression, thus behaving in counter–passive-aggressive ways.

This process of behaving in counter–passive-aggressive ways develops gradually; the passive-aggressive person's initial social behaviors are pleasant and appropriate. However, as the relationships become more active and personal, the passive-aggressive person becomes more frustrated and angry and behaves in passive-aggressive ways. As the Passive-Aggressive Conflict Cycle gains momentum, these passive-aggressive behaviors cause the targeted adult to experience similar feelings of anger. These feelings are never discussed by the adult (again, for simplicity's sake, we use "adult" as shorthand for the targeted person) in the relationship but become buried and expressed in counter–passive-aggressive behaviors. When this happens, the relationship moves into a new and more painful level of interaction.

The counter–passive-aggressive behavior of the adult creates new stress for the person, causing new angry feelings and more passive-aggressive behaviors. Likewise, the adult mirrors new feelings of anger and additional counter–passive-aggressive behaviors. This silent, interpersonal passive-aggressive struggle can continue for days, weeks, or months, but ultimately the adult cannot contain the anger and explodes by having a brief, intense temper tantrum.

Most adults we interviewed who were in passive-aggressive relationships were surprised at the intensity of their outbursts. These temper tantrums did not happen because the adult was emotionally unstable or lacked self-control. These adult temper tantrums are a predictable part of the psychology of passive aggression.

The Unconscious Accumulation of Counter-Aggressive Feelings

Over time, the adult unconsciously accumulates counter-aggressive feelings toward a passive-aggressive person. The counter-aggressive feelings increase in intensity and eventually erupt in a spontaneous outburst of aggression toward the passive-aggressive person. The infamous "Chinese water torture" is an appropriate analogy to use to explain this process.

In this form of torture, droplets of water are dripped onto the victim's forehead. Within a few days, the endless drip, drip, drip of water drives the victim to a state of madness. Each droplet of water by itself is harmless and tolerable. A single drop of water by itself does not cause psychological or physical harm. But if the water droplets are continuous, they will become intolerable and will plunge the victim into screaming lunacy. This analogy is extreme, but it serves to demonstrate what happens to adults over time when they are involved in passive-aggressive relationships.

Figure 10.3 uses a less extreme analogy—a water faucet dripping into a jar—to depict the long-term effects of a passive-aggressive behavior on an adult's temper. As you look at this figure, consider the following:

- Think of the dripping water as the intentional, subtle acts of a passive-aggressive person.

- Picture that as the drops settle into the jar, the passive-aggressive person disavows them, and they are transformed into angry feelings in an unsuspecting adult.

- *Keep in mind that the adult is not aware that the hidden anger is accumulating.* As time passes, the transferred anger may start to splash out as the adult experiences minor irritation or responds sarcastically toward the passive-aggressive person, but all along, the adult is not consciously aware of the process.

- Over time, the drips of water steadily continue to fill the jar and are quietly contained.

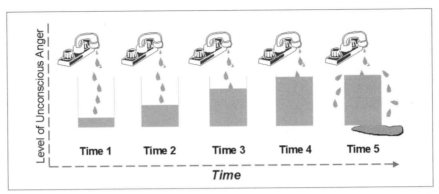

Figure 10.3. The accumulation over time of unconscious anger toward the person with a passive-aggressive personality. *Note.* From *The Angry Smile: Understanding and Managing Passive Aggressive Behavior of Students and Staff*, by N. J. Long, October 1998, paper presented at the Conflict Cycle Paradigm, KidsPeace National Center for Kids in Crisis, 16th National Conference, Allendale, PA. Copyright 1998 by KidsPeace. Reprinted with permission.

- At the overflow point, the adult experiences one more seemingly minor drip of passive-aggressive behavior from the person (e.g., "I didn't hear you. You need to speak louder"). This minor passive-aggressive act becomes the final droplet that floods the adult's capacity to control his or her accumulated counter-aggressive feelings.

- The adult's self-control dam breaks, and all the angry feelings accumulated toward the passive-aggressive person over the past weeks or months come flooding out in a cascade of emotional and irrational behavior. The adult yells, screams, threatens, swears, or even becomes physically violent toward the passive-aggressive person.

An outburst of anger is a predictable outcome for someone living with, teaching, or working with a passive-aggressive person. Because the adult is unaware of the unconscious accumulation of angry feelings toward the passive-aggressive person, this reaction will be repeated.

Justification of Passive-Aggressive Behavior After an Adult's Tantrum

After the adult has a temper tantrum (see Figure 10.4), the passive-aggressive person often responds by questioning the adult's emotional stability. Typical comments by the person with the original passive-aggressive behaviors include the following:

- "I don't know why you got so angry. I said I would clean it up later."

- "I thought you were my friend."

- "All I said was that the picture was hung crooked on the wall. I didn't yell, swear, hit, or break anything. But what you did was scary. I don't like to have someone blow up at me."

Figure 10.4. The successful temper tantrum.

- "I don't deserve to be yelled at in front of my colleagues. I think you overreacted to this situation and mistreated me. Don't you think you owe me an apology?"

The adult, who already feels guilty about the temper tantrum, feels terrible and usually ends up apologizing profusely. When this happens, the passive-aggressive recipient reluctantly accepts the apology on the condition that the adult will control his or her anger in the future. The adult usually agrees to these conditions, and the destructive interpersonal relationship continues until the adult's next explosive incident.

Validation of the Individual's Self-Fulfilling Prophecy

For a passive-aggressive person, anger in any form is perceived as a dangerous and destructive emotion that must be controlled. Once an adult assumes the angry feelings of the passive-aggressive person and behaviorally explodes, the angry tantrum provides the passive-aggressive person with visual evidence that he or she is fortunate to have his or her anger under control. The passive-aggressive person feels absolved from any wrongdoing and has no reason to give up his or her passive-aggressive way of relating to others. In fact, the adult's temper tantrum reinforces the passive-aggressive person's irrational beliefs about the danger of expressing anger and the importance of hiding it.

> For a passive-aggressive person, the normal expression of anger is a major source of anxiety because the person has never accepted his normal feelings of anger.

Overview of the Dynamics of Passive Aggression

To summarize the destructive interpersonal sequence of the Passive-Aggressive Conflict Cycle, we provide the following outline:

Initially, the adult is attracted to a passive-aggressive individual because of his or her social skills and nonaggressive manner.

As the relationship experiences a normal amount of frustration, the passive-aggressive individual begins to express anger in an indirect and subtle drip-by-drip manner. He or she may temporarily comply, forget, procrastinate, and so on.

The adult becomes irritated and confused by the behavior and begins to mirror it by becoming counter—passive aggressive. However, the adult is unaware of the amount of anger he or she is absorbing and accumulating from the passive-aggressive person. Over time, the adult's tolerance diminishes. Like a water glass that is filled to the top, the adult is psychologically filled and ready to spill over emotionally.

The next time the person responds in a passive-aggressive way to the adult's reasonable request, the adult explodes emotionally. An insignificant but irritating behavior by the passive-aggressive person becomes the final drip that spills the water, the spark that lights the fuse, the proverbial straw that breaks the camel's back.

Suddenly, the adult experiences a brief but intense temper tantrum. During this time, the adult yells, screams, throws things, curses, or even hits the passive-aggressive person.

The person reacts to the adult's aggressive behavior with shock and alarm and thinks, for example, "Wow! Look how crazy people get when they express their anger directly. I can't believe she is so angry and out of control over such an insignificant incident! Isn't it fortunate that I have learned a more effective way of controlling my anger so that my anger does not control *me*!"

Once the adult has calmed down, he or she usually feels very upset and guilty for overreacting to such a minor incident. The adult not only feels sorry for losing all semblance of self-control but also thinks, "I'm a terrible person. What is wrong with me?"

Simultaneously, the passive-aggressive person tells the adult that he or she does not deserve to be victimized, that the adult's behavior was an overreaction to a minor incident, and that he or she deserves an immediate apology.

The adult agrees and apologizes, saying, "I don't know what came over me. I'm sorry. It won't happen again."

This apology has a special psychological meaning to the passive-aggressive person. It reinforces the person's belief that the expression of anger is dangerous and destructive. Consequently, the person has no motivation to alter his or her passive-aggressive way of life.

Sadly the adult continues the emotional roller-coaster bond with the passive-aggressive person until the next temper tantrum occurs.

This pattern of behavior will perpetuate itself until the adult becomes aware of his or her accumulated anger and finds appropriate ways of expressing that anger in nontoxic ways.

Examples of the Passive-Aggressive Conflict Cycle

The most valuable aspects of both the Conflict Cycle and the Passive-Aggressive Conflict Cycle are their infinite usability and applicability to conflict situations.

Grounded in cognitive and behavioral theory, the Conflict Cycle paradigms are also real-world, practical models. For years, we have encouraged our adult training participants to learn and apply the conflict cycles in their professional work. At the same time, we have taught the models to children and youth, teaching them step by step how their thoughts, feelings, behaviors, and the resulting reactions of others fueled repetitive and no-win power struggles. Many an "A-ha!" moment has been achieved through a discussion of the paradigm with intelligent adults and troubled children.

The following examples demonstrate the applicability of the Passive-Aggressive Conflict Cycle in everyday settings: home, school, close adult relationships, and the workplace.

In the Home

"The boy was just hungry"

I was preparing for a dinner party one evening for my husband's boss. I worked all day cleaning the house, making the table look beautiful, and organizing a fancy dinner. I had almost everything under control when my son, Alex, age 15, and my daughter, Bethany, age 17, arrived home from school. Alex was in his typical passive-aggressive mode. He walked in and dumped his jacket on the floor. I clearly stated, "Alex, please hang up your coat, pronto. I'm having Dad's boss and wife over for dinner and have picked up the house all day." Alex replied, "In a minute, I'm dying of thirst," as he rushed to the spotless kitchen and opened the refrigerator, taking out a large bottle of Coke, the jelly, peanut butter, and bread. I watched in dismay as he spilled Coke and splattered crumbs across the counter as he carried his messy snack to the breakfast nook, but I said little because my growing son needed fuel. As he slowly finished eating, I said, "Okay, Alex, clean up your mess now." He replied, "Sure, sure, just as soon as I go to the bathroom." There he tarried until I had to knock on the door and request his immediate help.

Alex was sulking and carrying his unfinished Coke as he opened the door. He placed the dripping glass on a pile of homework abandoned in the kitchen by Bethany. The glass produced a huge wet ring on Bethany's research report and I screamed, "No, not there, you idiot!" He looked at me in a perplexed way, and asked, "Why do you get so angry over little things? What kind of mother are you, some kind of witch?" I then lost it completely and slapped Alex across the cheek. He was stunned and said, "I don't need your abuse."

With tears of guilt and a shaky hand, I dialed my husband's office and told him about the upsetting series of events. My husband was not very sympathetic. He said, "Gosh, Ann, all he needed was some food and the bathroom after school. That doesn't sound so unreasonable to me. You seem to have overreacted to his behavior." I hung up and went to my bathtub for bubbles and a good cry.

At School

The teacher is a caring and compassionate person who becomes programmed by a 6-year-old passive-aggressive student named Mario. Notice how the teacher's behavior follows this sequence and how she inadvertently empowers Mario to become more passive aggressive by telling the class that they will not be able to leave or have their recess until Mario completes his task. The original intent was to put group pressure on Mario, but what she did was to turn over control of the class to her passive-aggressive student. Finally she explodes, grabs Mario, and then feels guilty. Even though this example takes place in a school with a young student, this pattern exists with all ages and in all settings.

Over the Edge

Children affect teachers in a variety of ways. Some are precocious, yet appealing. Some are shy and introverted, yet appealing. And some do everything wrong, yet somehow there exists a special affection between teacher and child. Mario, a 6-year-old with a learning disability, did not fit into any of these categories. The only way I can describe Mario is by using the terms *inconsistent* and *frumpy*. Yet the more I observed him, the more intellectually capable I realized he was. However, Mario never quite got all of the directions straight or completed a task "in toto." When I questioned him about his lack of concentration, he would give me a half smile that would just about send me through the ceiling. It was incredible the way Mario got under my skin. When he was messing around, I wouldn't lose my temper; I would merely say to the rest of the group, "We can't go out to recess until Mario finishes his lesson." Everyone would look back at Mario and groan. Writing about this makes me feel even more guilty than I felt then, because at that time I could defensively justify my reasons for doing something that I now am able to recognize as so counter–passive aggressive.

Mario and I had successive incidents, and we learned to play the game of passive aggression quite well. However, I was unaware that my hostility and anger were mounting day by day. The seepage continued through November, and one day in December, it exploded!

It happened like this. At 2:35, the children were asked to go quietly for their coats, line up, and be out of the door at 2:45. Mario was always the last one to get his coat. There were many times when he would give me a half smile and tell me he couldn't find his coat. My most common answer was to ask another child, for example, "Mary, since Mario is unable to recognize his own coat, would you find it for him so that we can leave?" My tone would be incredibly sarcastic. Again, the children would groan.

On this particular Monday, I was in a hurry to have the children leave because I had an exam scheduled at 5:00 at American University. I am sure the children sensed my haste, because I would tell them about my graduate classes, tests, papers, and so on. At 2:40, everyone had their coats on and were lined up . . . except Mario. He was sitting reading a book. I couldn't believe it! I called sternly, "Mario, go get your coat!" He looked up at me with his half smile as though I was speaking Chinese. I started to march to his seat with steam pouring out of me, but I stopped and had the presence of mind to dismiss the group. "Mario, for God's sake get your coat!" I screamed. My voice was angry, and my teeth were clenched as I spoke. He continued to look at me as if I was crazy, seemingly not understanding. Finally I grabbed him by the arm and applied pressure, as I pulled him toward the coat rack. He began to whimper. At that point I couldn't decide whether I wanted to smack him or comfort him. I did experience tremendous sorrow for the both of us and released the grip on his arm and placed my hand gently around his head as he sobbed. I had acted on my feelings and not on a professional level. I was more concerned about my needs than trying to help Mario meet his needs.

In Close Adult Relationships

"It must be your eating disorder"

Though we have been married for 20 years, my husband and I are true opposites. He's a night owl; I like to rise with the sun. He has been overweight for most of our marriage; I have remained thin. He never yells or shows his anger; I wear my emotions on my sleeve. These last two differences converged in one major scene at a family reunion dinner party last week.

Though it might sound unusual to complain about "thin jokes," I have realized that, because they are much more socially acceptable than a "fat joke" would ever be, my husband has gotten away with publicly making them in a mean-spirited way for years! If we dine together, I can count on him to scrutinize everything I put on my plate and to make critical comments about my choices—something I would never do to him. Taken alone, his jabs could seem humorous, but over the course of a meal, they add up to real insults.

Last week, we were at a restaurant with 30 family members celebrating the end of a reunion weekend. When the waiter placed my drink in front of me, my husband announced loudly, "You're drinking a diet soda? It must be your eating disorder kicking in again!" Instantly, all eyes were on me and I could feel the mix of tension, judgment, doubt, and pity at the table. I snapped.

"You're the one who needs to cut the calories!" I shouted, surprised at the loudness of my own voice. "Why don't you drink it?" I slammed the drink so hard at his place setting that it splattered all over both of us. Humiliated, I stormed off to the ladies' room. I heard my husband call after me, "Honey, it was just a joke. I was kidding!"

When I returned to the table minutes later, I was cleaned up but still shaken. I politely apologized to my family and sat feeling ashamed and embarrassed for the rest of the meal. I knew the lasting impression I had made on my extended family was that of a high-strung lunatic and that my overreaction to my husband's comment probably convinced everyone that I did, in fact, have an eating disorder.

To top it all off, when I angrily confronted my husband after the party, he staunchly defended his joke and told me I was overreacting. In a relighting of my fuse, he even suggested that if I was so sensitive about my weight, maybe I really did have an eating disorder. I swear, for a moment I even doubted myself.

After the Angry Smile seminar, a light came on. I understood my husband's behaviors in the light of the Passive-Aggressive Conflict Cycle and realized that I had been allowing his depreciating comments to become my problem. I could see that because I had been the punchline of so many of my husband's unkind jokes that reunion weekend, his seemingly minor "humorous" implication that I was suffering from a psychiatric disorder turned into an embarrassing, major overreaction on my part. In what I now recognize as clear passive aggression, he disguised his public insult as humor and fended me off successfully with his defensive outrage to my angry confrontation.

In the Workplace

Explosion in the Boardroom

I had been partnered on a project at work for months with a very passive-aggressive man. He took every opportunity to be late for scheduled appointments with customers, which made me look personally foolish, embarrassed our company, and sabotaged our meeting objectives. He was also habitually late filing reports, which meant that I either had to take the joint blame for their tardiness or do double the workload to get them in on time. I was annoyed by his actions but took them all in stride, knowing that when the project was completed, I would be free to work on my own again.

When the job was finished, we had a department meeting to summarize our results. Though I had ended up doing 95% of the work to prepare our presentation, my passive-aggressive partner suddenly came to life in the meeting and quite literally stole the show. He assumed responsibility for all of our accomplishments and minimized—even belittled—my contributions. I bit my tongue for the first half hour but when he started to recount a customer meeting that he had never even shown up for, I cracked under the pressure. With the full department as my audience, I lashed out at his nonparticipation throughout the months and called him names that would be inappropriate even outside of our boardroom. While the thrashing felt great for the first half minute, I felt the support of my peers drain as I continued. My anger drove me, though, and I couldn't find a place to stop. My boss did it for me, asking me to leave the room and meet him in his office.

In the end, I got a tongue-lashing of my own at the hands of my boss, who was "surprised and appalled" at my outburst. The hard work and professionalism I had applied to the project was completely undone by my childish explosion in the meeting. Worst yet, my passive-aggressive partner, who had contributed nothing to the work objectives, had calmly positioned himself as the rational, tolerant office superstar.

What these examples of the Passive-Aggressive Conflict Cycle have in common is that the mother, teacher, wife, and business partner were all unaware of the psychology of passive aggression as they carried on their interactions. By not recognizing or assigning weight to the subtle signs, minor irritations, or initial spins of the Passive-Aggressive Conflict Cycle, they became programmed to behave toward their passive-aggressive counterparts in predictable, escalating sequences. Once their counter-aggressive feelings exploded into impulsive and inappropriate behavior, the conflict escalated into a lose–win situation that included feeling guilty for their atypical aggressive outbursts. These four examples are classic descriptions of how reasonable adults who have chronic relationships with passive-aggressive people become trapped in the dynamics of the Passive-Aggressive Conflict Cycle.

When Both People Have Passive-Aggressive Personalities

Does a passive-aggressive person ever have an impulse breakthrough like the targeted adult? This is one frequently asked question from our seminar participants. Based on our experience, the answer is *almost never*, assuming the passive-aggressive person selects as his or her target an adult who is not passive aggressive.

The exception to this interpretation is when *both* persons are passive aggressive. In the case of a parent–child passive-aggressive dynamic, the playing field is tilted toward the parent. The parent is older, has more authority and status than the child, and usually has had more experience perfecting passive-aggressive skills. The child cannot control the relationship. Under these psychological conditions, a chronic passive-aggressive power struggle occurs between them and, over time, the outcome favors the parent. The same is true for any of the other settings we have examined (in school, in a close adult relationship, at work)—when two passive-aggressive persons engage, the one who holds more power (however that is determined in the relationship) will be more tenacious and successful in creating lose–win situations for the other.

Summary

The Passive-Aggressive Conflict Cycle is our paradigm for explaining how rational, straightforward, assertive adults can momentarily and unexpectedly depart from their typical personas and take on inappropriate, childlike, and unprofessional behaviors. Combined with the explanation of counter–passive aggression, the model describes the psychology of passive aggression and predicts the endless, repetitive cycles of conflict that gain momentum when an unsuspecting adult's reservoir of accumulated anger floods its banks.

In this chapter, we described the predictable sequence of the Passive-Aggressive Conflict Cycle, highlighting each of its five stages. This essential point was emphasized: The targeted adult is unaware of his or her accumulation of counter-aggressive feelings toward the passive-aggressive person. When the adult's emotions eventually overflow in the form of a brief but intense adult tantrum, the adult ends up feeling both guilty and ashamed. The out-of-control tantrum and the painful emotions that follow create the reinforcement that the passive-aggressive person needs—confirming that anger is a dangerous emotion and should be hidden at all times.

In Chapters 11 and 12, you will learn how to halt the Passive-Aggressive Conflict Cycle before its vicious spins permanently damage relationships and ultimately reinforce irrational beliefs. Skills for altering ineffective responses to passive aggression are defined and the process of Benign Confrontation is detailed.

Changing Responses to Passive-Aggressive Behavior

11

If dealing with passive-aggressive behavior were easy, you wouldn't struggle with it, and we wouldn't need to write about it. Passive-aggressive behavior is difficult. It confounds professional classification, it confuses both competent parents and seasoned teachers, and it often blindsides unsuspecting spouses and undeserving coworkers. In this book, we present a new theory of passive aggression. Our approach acknowledges the complexity of passive-aggressive behavior and offers specific skills and steps for meeting its challenges.

What we offer is not a miracle cure or one-time treatment but rather an intervention approach grounded in theory and rooted in more than 40 years of clinical and educational experience. Prior to this publication, there were insufficient professional guidelines for managing passive-aggressive behavior in the home, school, in close adult relationships, and in the workplace. Parents, teachers, spouses, and coworkers were on their own to do whatever they thought was helpful at the time. Probably the most frequent reaction from a frustrated adult was to yell, "Don't let me tell you again! Do it now!" Their words were loud and clear, but the message was ineffective.

Adults no longer have to rely on their authority or participate in chronic struggles with individuals who are passive aggressive. To improve relationships and deescalate conflict cycles, we provide specific short- and long-term intervention skills. These skills are grouped based on two outcome goals:

1. changing responses to passive-aggressive behavior

2. changing the passive-aggressive behavior itself

The second goal will be addressed in Chapter 12, as the steps of Benign Confrontation of passive-aggressive behavior are taught. In this chapter, we define eight specific skills for changing one's responses to passive-aggressive behavior.

Before any true and lasting change can take place in a person's behavior, the rewards for that behavior must be eliminated. The eight skills we identify for changing one's responses to passive-aggressive behavior provide insight and instruction for how adults can take away the reinforcement that a person experiences from his or her passive-aggressive behavior. When this intervention piece is combined with the Benign Confrontation approach, the person who once relied on passive-aggressive behavior as a way of life is led to new, healthier patterns of emotional expression.

Eight Skills for Changing Responses to Passive-Aggressive Behavior

The eight skills for changing one's responses to passive-aggressive behavior can be broken down into several groups. As you read, consider the first four skills as tools of self-awareness and self-management. Note that Skills 1 and 2 are essential prerequisites for the completion of all of the other identified skills. The final four skills are grouped as effective responses to the most common passive-aggressive behaviors.

Skills 1–4: Self-Awareness and Self-Management

Skill 1: Recognize the Warning Signs of Passive Aggression

To be forewarned is to be forearmed. Once you are familiar with the characteristics of passive-aggressive behavior (see Table 11.1), you can avoid being a naïve and unwitting victim of a person's predictable and destructive way of engaging you. Further, with the ability to recognize the five distinct levels of passive-aggressive behavior and the knowledge of the Passive-Aggressive Conflict Cycle, you gain the competence to disengage from the person emotionally and to avoid reinforcing his or her passive-aggressive behavior.

One of the greatest threats of passive-aggressive behavior is how the targeted adult becomes emotionally flooded and worn down before even realizing that passive-aggressive dynamics are in play. The ability to recognize passive-aggressive behaviors as they are occurring and to continuously monitor the feelings they create is critical to effectively managing responses.

> One of the greatest threats of passive-aggressive behavior is how the targeted adult becomes emotionally flooded and worn down before even realizing that passive-aggressive dynamics are in play.

Skill 2: Acknowledge and Accept Your Own Angry Feelings

Being able to acknowledge your normal feelings of anger is a cognitive self-talk skill. It is healthy to be able to accept feelings of anger as real, potent, and important to your life. It is essential to be able to say "yes" to the presence of anger and "no" to the expression of that anger through aggressive or passive-aggressive acts. The skills of self-awareness and self-talk are essential to changing your responses to passive-aggressive behavior. They provide powerful insight into the person's

Table II.I

Common Passive-Aggressive Behavior Patterns

Denies anger

Resents authority

Procrastinates

Gives excessive excuses

Claims forgetfulness or misunderstanding

Keeps others waiting and dangling

Is intentionally inefficient

Acts evasive and secretive at times

Uses the silent treatment

Shuts down conversations with "Fine" and "Whatever"

Is often charming and intelligent

Gives out hidden, coded messages, drip by drip

Acts pleasant one week, intolerable the next week, making you feel you're on a perpetual emotional roller coaster

Brings out temper tantrums and feelings of guilt in others

unexpressed anger while protecting you from internalizing the person's angry feelings and behaviors.

For example, if you call a child to dinner or ask a student to share a report and she does not respond, you probably will ask her again. But if you have to ask her a third time and she still does not respond, you should immediately think, "passive aggressive." Simultaneously, you should say the following to yourself:

> "I've just identified this as passive-aggressive behavior. She wants me to get angry and yell at her, so it will end up being my problem and not hers. I will not participate in this unproductive passive-aggressive game. I know what is behind her overt behavior of deafness. It is her feelings of anger and resentment that she is unable to express to me openly."

Whereas specific developmental pathways (see Chapter 2) lead a person to fear and disavow his or her anger, healthy adult emotional expression relies on the acceptance of a full range of feelings. In our Life Space Crisis Intervention training, we teach that youth in crisis don't so much *have* feelings but rather are *had* by their feelings. The same is true for persons who never learn to "make friends" with their anger; instead of learning to control their feelings, they spend a lifetime having their feelings control them.

It is predictable that even for the most assertive and emotionally healthy adult, keeping one's anger under control can at times be a challenge. The following self-talk strategies are proposed to help you manage your counter–passive-aggressive feelings under three different stressful situations with a passive-aggressive person:

1. When You Know You Will Be Meeting a Passive-Aggressive Person

This is the time to *anticipate the interactions* and practice saying the following to yourself:

- "I will not let him push my emotional buttons. I know in advance what he will do to frustrate me."

- "This will be a challenging situation, but I can handle it because I am aware of her underlying anger."

- "I will develop a definite plan and a scripted response to his passive-aggressive behaviors. Then I will know what to say and do in advance when he behaves passive aggressively."

- "I will be in control of this situation when we meet."

2. When You Are Relating to a Passive-Aggressive Person and Are Becoming Upset

This is the time to *recognize the warning signs* and say the following to yourself:

- "Stop. Stay calm. Count to 15."

- "I need to identify my feelings of anger but not become counter–passive aggressive, because it will make the situation worse."

- "I will not yell or become sarcastic, because this behavior will only escalate the conflict."

- "Remember, I am in touch with my underlying feelings of anger, and she is not. I have total choice over how I express my angry feelings in behavior. She doesn't."

- "There is no need to doubt myself, because I can see beyond his irritating passive-aggressive behavior and recognize his fear of anger."

- "I recognize what she is trying to do to me, but I can get through it."

3. When You Are Relating to a Passive-Aggressive Person and Are About to Explode

This is the time to acknowledge and accept your own anger and say the following:

- "I know what is happening. My counter-aggressive feelings are becoming intense. I need to deescalate them."

- "If I explode, it will only reinforce his irrational beliefs about anger and make my life miserable."

- "I will instruct myself to lower my tone and volume and to speak more slowly."

- "I will assert myself by sending an 'I' message (e.g., 'I am having difficulty dealing with your behavior right now. I need to sort out my feelings. We need to discuss this situation, but not right now. I need to stop this conversation, but later I want the opportunity to share with you my thoughts about our relationship’).”

- “Now I will walk away quickly and with confidence.”

These three cognitive self-talk strategies are useful anger-management skills and have four personal advantages. They will

1. stop the accumulation of unconscious anger that we discussed in Chapter 9,

2. prevent you from having an emotional meltdown when your unconscious anger reaches flood level,

3. protect you from your subsequent feelings of guilt if you have an emotional temper tantrum, and

4. eliminate the expression of your aggressive behavior, which the person uses to justify his or her behavior and belief that the expression of anger is dangerous.

Skill 3: Manage Personal Anger and Role-Model Assertive Behavior

The Passive-Aggressive Conflict Cycle demonstrates how a person’s passive-aggressive behaviors create in adults not only the person’s angry feelings but also counter–passive-aggressive behaviors. Remember, the adult rarely initiates a Passive-Aggressive Conflict Cycle but often behaves in a way that will perpetuate it.

Once this happens, the adult needs to stop all of the “you” messages, which promote counter–passive-aggressive behaviors, and rephrase thoughts as “I” messages. What’s more, in dealing with passive-aggressive behavior and rising angry feelings, it is often helpful to acknowledge the difficulty of the situation and to request a break from it. Taking time away allows your body to cool off physiologically and role-models for the passive-aggressive person that you are in control of when and how you will express your feelings. The following response is an example of a helpful “I” message:

“I am becoming upset, and I need to stop and understand why I am feeling angry. Perhaps this is something you need to think about too.”

Though we have focused on the knee-jerk mirroring of poor behavior, as in the Passive-Aggressive Conflict Cycle, it is essential to capitalize on the opportunity that adults have to purposefully behave in constructive ways that they want their children, students, spouses, or coworkers to copy. Every time an adult uses assertive “I” messages and conscientiously expresses anger in direct, emotionally honest ways, he or she stops the Passive-Aggressive Conflict Cycle in its tracks and role-models a better way to behave. The power of role-modeling is second to none; in aiming to change a person’s passive-aggressive behavior, modeling assertive responses is a nonnegotiable prerequisite.

A psychological truism is that one cannot control or create lasting change in another person’s behavior by doing something to that person. Rather, one can only alter his or her own responses to the person and anticipate that behavioral change will occur because the undesired behavior is no longer being reinforced by the old response. Each time passive-aggressive behavior is answered with a mirrored counter–passive-aggressive response, the hidden means of expressing anger is reinforced, and an opportunity for direct emotional expression is lost. On the other hand, each time passive-aggressive behavior is met with assertiveness, through "I" messages and Benign Confrontation (see Chapter 12), the hidden anger is weakened.

Remembering the water jar analogy from Chapter 10, consider that each time passive aggression is met with assertiveness, a drop of water is siphoned off from the bottom of the jar. Now, in contrast to the jar filling up to flood level, the jar is emptied, drop by drop. Over time, the consistent nonreinforcement of passive-aggressive behaviors allows the jar of anger to drain completely. What's more, when the passive-aggressive person realizes that he or she cannot cause the other person to store up and act out angry feelings, he or she is forced to relate to the person on a different, more emotionally honest, level. When counter–passive-aggressive responses are eliminated, the passive-aggressive person's behavior is effectively altered.

Skill 4: Avoid Empowering a Passive-Aggressive Person

Passive-aggressive persons are empowered when they are allowed to assume control over a situation. In the following examples, well-intentioned statements backfired and inadvertently handed the power to the passive-aggressive person:

- A mother says to her daughter Hayley's siblings, "We can't go to the movie until Hayley feeds the dog."

- A teacher says to a class, "Everyone will have to stop all activity until Leroy gets off the floor."

- A wife says to a spouse, "We won't sit down for dinner until you turn off that TV."

- A supervisor says to a work team, "Bonus checks will be withheld until Jackie turns in the final section of her report."

In each of these examples, an adult inadvertently gives a passive-aggressive person the power to control the situation and influence the immediate comfort and pleasure of others. While the original intent of each adult's comment was to create group pressure on Hayley, Leroy, the spouse, or Jackie to get them to conform, the result is that these passive-aggressive children, students, spouses and coworkers think, "Thank you, now I can delay and procrastinate and frustrate the whole group." Consequently, instead of solving the problem, the adult has escalated it!

If an adult makes the mistake of empowering a passive-aggressive person, the damage can be undone. For example, the adult can reverse the situation by saying, "I have thought it over, and I've decided to change my mind. We can all go, but Leroy will have to stay." This immediately repositions the power and control from the passive-aggressive person to the adult.

The next four skills for changing responses to passive-aggressive behavior provide instruction and guidance for how to respond to some of the most common passive-aggressive behaviors exhibited at home, at school, in close adult relationships, and in the workplace.

Skills 5–8: Effective Responses

Skill 5: Responding to Temporary Deafness: *The Columbo Technique*

When a passive-aggressive person who is feigning temporary deafness is identified, we suggest using the technique made famous by Detective Columbo, from the classic TV show starring Peter Falk. Rather than using an angry, in-your-face crime-fighting approach, Lieutenant Columbo cleverly engages suspects through his deferential, unassuming manner. When they do not feel threatened or backed into a corner, his suspects let down their guard and give Columbo the information or response he is after.

The same approach works wonders with passive-aggressive persons. A teacher using this skill for responding to temporary deafness reported the following results:

> After three requests with no response, I approached Sam, a passive-aggressive student in my class. I looked at the ceiling and spoke in a soft voice—as if I was talking to myself but still loud enough that Sam could hear me. "Isn't this interesting?" I commented. "I asked Sam to get the book off the table, and he pretended he didn't hear me. I know he can hear. I think I'll ask him one more time and see what he does." Then, I looked Sam straight in the eyes and said, "Sam, will you please get me the encyclopedia, letter M, from the back of the room?" My act worked! Sam got the book right away.

In almost all cases, the person will complete the task immediately. In a calm and nonaccusatory manner, the adult simply stated the facts to the student and let the student respond from there. This calm demeanor and refusal to argue was probably quite disarming to Sam, who was most likely expecting an authoritarian, angry, or counter–passive-aggressive response from his teacher. By using a Columbo-esque feigned naïveté, the teacher failed to reinforce the passive-aggressive façade of temporary deafness and instead succeeded in getting Sam to respond positively.

Passive-aggressive youth have shared with us their belief that "adults are naïve and stupid, and it is easy to trick them into believing we don't hear them." As Detective Columbo taught us over so many episodes, a laid-back, pondering technique can be quite disarming and highly effective in eliciting a desired response.

Skill 6: Responding Differently to Feigned Misunderstanding: *Setting Clear Expectations*

Feigned misunderstanding masks passive aggression behind a veil of sincerity.

- When you ask your son to cut the grass and he goes outside only to return an hour later without completing his chore, do not be surprised if he says, "I didn't know you wanted me to do it right away."

- When you tell a passive-aggressive student her report has to be 10 pages and she hands in only 3, know what you are dealing with when she says, "I was sure you said the report only had to be 3 pages."

- When you ask your wife to pick up a box of Whole Wheat Crispies for you at the grocery store and she returns with a box of Sugar O's, a red flag should go up when she says, "Oh! I could have sworn this was the brand you liked!"

- When you ask your boss to schedule the staff picnic for a day you are in town and he announces to everyone that it will take place on the date of your most important out-of-state conference, do not be surprised when he says, "Oh, sorry. I thought it was the following week."

These examples illustrate how a passive-aggressive person commonly justifies his or her hidden angry agenda by feigning misunderstanding. Going head to head against these justifications will be a losing battle—guaranteed. Based on the very nature of their personality style, passive-aggressive people have a great deal invested in maintaining their façade and keeping their angry intentions under wraps. Further, the person will only gain pleasure and satisfaction in watching your anger mount as you try to counter his or her endless, maddening excuses. The passive-aggressive person will "win" on both counts while you lose twice—lashing out angrily and still not having the task completed.

So while there is little chance of making a passive-aggressive person "admit" that his or her behavior is purposeful or unacceptable, there is hope for the adult who is up against feigned misunderstanding. The skill of managing this type of passive-aggressive behavior is to set crystal-clear expectations at the very outset of the interaction and to never assume that a passive-aggressive person understands your request. Even if the task you are assigning is routine and has been carried out many times in the past, be sure to review your precise expectations for quantity, quality, deadlines, dates, brands, parameters, and so forth with the person ahead of time. Better still, provide your request in writing so that you always have a paper trail to fall back on.

Do not allow sarcasm or condescension in your voice as you detail the request; the passive-aggressive person will understand this tone as counter–passive aggression, which will fuel another passive-aggressive conflict cycle and thwart your own efforts. Rather, make your expectations as clear as possible in a neutral, assertive tone.

In the short term, stating clear expectations will prevent many of the issues presented by feigned misunderstanding. Over the long term, if you hope to one day avoid spelling out every expectation, a more in-depth confrontation of the person's underlying anger will need to take place. The skills of Benign Confrontation are useful for achieving this type of lasting change.

Skill 7: Responding Differently to Chronically Late Behavior: *Taking Away Secondary Gratification*

A person who is habitually late coming home, arriving at school, attending scheduled family activities, or showing up at meetings may be indirectly expressing anger toward people or events. Habitual lateness not only frustrates others but also provides passive-aggressive persons with secondary gratification as they realize they don't have to meet others' schedules and expectations and can believe that their time is more important than that of others. Likewise, the passive-aggressive person is gratified when a person or group's progress is delayed due to their lateness. Never allow a passive-aggressive person to hold an individual or group hostage to his or her angry timetable.

The skill of dealing with this type of behavior includes setting clear limits and taking away any secondary gratification the person may receive by being late. When, for example, you tell your teenager that she should be home on Friday night by 11:00 P.M. and she arrives home at midnight, do not argue with her or get into a long discussion about her excuses for being late. Say, "You decided not to be home at the agreed-upon time, so we are choosing for you to come home at 10:30 next weekend."

This is one of the few times where any further discussion with the teenager will only lead to an increased power struggle. If your teenager tries to argue, do not take the bait. Remaining calm and not taking on her anger is the most effective way to disengage from the Passive-Aggressive Conflict Cycle and to disarm the power of her hidden anger. Remember to follow through with limits.

Skill 8: Responding Differently to Delay Behaviors: *Establishing Logical Consequences*

Passive-aggressive delay behavior is a form of procrastination—that faithful "friend" that we mentioned in Chapter 1. While the desire to put off tasks we don't feel like completing is universal, the passive-aggressive person has an additional underlying agenda: to covertly inspire anger in a targeted adult. In general, the more the person delays, the angrier the adult becomes. Also, by responding in sluggish ways, the passive-aggressive person aims to control a situation by slowing down whatever needs to be done. Common examples of how passive-aggressive persons employ delay behaviors include the following:

- A mother asks her son to clean his room before his sister's soccer game, and he says, "Don't worry, I'll clean it sometime this morning," secretly hoping to make the family late for the game.

- A teacher asks a student if she has completed her book report and she answers, "I'll do it after I read this chapter," knowing that the bell will ring before she is finished reading.

- A wife asks her husband to take out the recycling bin before the collection truck comes and he says, "I'll do it after my shower," knowing that the truck is just three houses away.

- An employee asks his boss to write a letter of reference and the boss agrees but does not get around to it until the employee notices that the letter is conspicuously missing from his file.

As with feigned misunderstanding and chronic lateness, the critical first skill for handling delay behaviors is to establish precise limits and deadlines. Second, it is important to take away the gratification that the passive-aggressive person receives from his or her delay tactics. If the person sees that he or she is successful in holding up an entire group, not having to complete a chore, or eliciting an angry response, the passive-aggressive person feels that his or her objectives have been met and the behavior is reinforced. Third, the passive-aggressive person needs to know that clear, natural consequences exist for his or her delay behaviors. In this way, the person experiences accountability and pays an uncomfortable price for his or her actions. When these three skills are implemented, much changes for the passive-aggressive person:

1. Excuses such as "I didn't know" are no longer plausible.

2. The pleasure of controlling a situation and inciting anger is eliminated.

3. Behavioral accountability is experienced.

In the first two aforementioned examples, the parent and the teacher have some natural leverage to implement these skills, given the authority of their role. For example, the mother can say to her son,

"Okay, let's agree that you will clean up your room by noon. I need all of your dirty clothes in the hamper and your bed made neatly. If you do this, you can go to the mall. If you don't, you choose to stay home until it is completed."

Likewise, the teacher can say to his student,

"Let's agree that your report will be completed by the end of this period. If you do it, you are free to follow your schedule. If you don't, you choose to write the report in the study hall during recess."

Notice that in both of these examples, the passive-aggressive person is made responsible for his or her own behavior.

The task of holding a passive-aggressive person accountable becomes more challenging in the last two examples, when adults face other adults and the power dynamic does not afford the same leverage as the parent–child or teacher–student dynamic. In the first chapter, we defined anger-related terms and made distinctions between passive, aggressive, passive-aggressive, and assertive responses. Let's revisit these terms to gain insight into how to respond effectively to delay behaviors in adult relationships.

Scenario: A wife asks her husband to take out the recycling bin before the collection truck comes and he says, "I'll do it after my shower," knowing that the truck is just three houses away.

Wife's *passive* response: "OK, honey. No problem." (She knows the truck will pass by and their recycling bin will remain full for another week.)

Wife's *aggressive* response: "I'll do it myself! Just make sure you don't ask me for any favors!"

Wife's *counter–passive-aggressive* response: "Fine." (When her husband is in the shower, she runs all the hot water in the house, knowing this will give him an ice cold shower.)

Wife's *assertive* response: "I'd like you to do it now before the truck passes our house. I can see it three houses down the road. If you shower first, you'll miss the pick up for the week and then you'll have to take it to the dumpster."

Though the wife does not have the clear-cut authority of a parent or teacher, nor does she choose to pressure her husband with a costly consequence, her assertive communication style still effectively counters his passive-aggressive delay behavior. This type of clear, direct, emotionally neutral statement of needs is important in any response to passive-aggressive behavior, but especially among adults when the power dynamic does not favor one or the other.

In the fourth example, when the balance of power actually favors the passive-aggressive boss, the employee must take extra care to maintain his assertiveness while vigilantly communicating expectations, minimizing opportunities for secondary gratification, and creating consequences:

> **Scenario:** An employee asks his boss to write a letter of reference and the boss agrees but does not get around to it until the employee notices that the letter is conspicuously missing from his file.

> **Expectations:** The employee should give his boss the deadline for the letter of reference in writing and follow up the initial request with an e-mail or second written reminder.

> **Gratification:** If he knows that his boss is often passive aggressive and typically uses delay tactics (Skill 1: Know What You Are Dealing With), the employee should have a backup reference who will be willing to write a letter. Though a direct boss is desirable, often a representative from human resources, a former supervisor, a boss further up the chain of command, or a coworker is a perfectly acceptable (and sometimes more favorable) substitute. The goal is for the employee to cover his bases so that his passive-aggressive boss does not experience the gratification of controlling the situation by delaying the reference letter.

> **Consequences:** While most employees don't hold a great amount of leverage over their bosses, what the employee can do is communicate his request ahead of time to human resources or to his boss' boss, just as an FYI. In that way, the boss is held accountable because others are aware that he has been asked to complete the task.

Scenarios abound and the possibilities for changed responses to passive-aggressive behavior are as varied as the situation. The good news is that these skills are effective at helping people disengage from the Passive-Aggressive Conflict Cycle most of the time. The challenge is that these skills will have to be used time and again with the passive-aggressive person because they only address the surface-level, situation-specific issue. To effect real, lasting change, the root of the underlying anger must be addressed, as we will see in Chapter 12.

Summary

In this chapter, we have focused on short-term intervention skills for managing passive-aggressive behavior at home, in school, in close adult relationships, and in the workplace. Eight specific skills give instruction on how a person on the receiving end of passive aggression can respond effectively and avoid becoming caught up in the Passive-Aggressive Conflict Cycle (see Table 11.2). These assertive responses

Table 11.2

Rules for Responding to Passive-Aggressive Behaviors

1. Recognize passive-aggressive behaviors as they are acted out.

2. Acknowledge and accept your own angry feelings.

3. Manage personal anger and role-model assertive behavior.

4. End all empowerment of passive aggression.

5. Maintain a calm, nonthreatening stance.

6. Establish and enforce precise limits.

7. Minimize opportunities for secondary gratification.

8. Employ logical, natural consequences.

aim to stop hidden anger in its tracks and disarm its power. In Chapter 12, we explore the long-term strategy of unmasking hidden anger and helping the passive-aggressive person change his or her pathological behavior, using the step-by-step process of Benign Confrontation.

Benign Confrontation of Passive-Aggressive Behavior

Over the years, our seminar participants have been fascinated by the passive-aggressive personality type and challenged by the various levels at which the behavior is displayed at home, in school, in close adult relationships, and at work. As a parent or a professional who is on the receiving end of passive-aggressive behavior, it is unlikely that you have escaped the experience of counter–passive aggression because you have no doubt taken a spin along the Passive-Aggressive Conflict Cycle once or twice in your life.

The skill of Benign Confrontation is an effective but challenging process. While most people relate to the facts, scenarios, and emotions presented in this book, eagerness to take on the final skill set of Benign Confrontation is a different story. For many, confrontation is a scary prospect. Whether out of fear of receiving a person's anger or out of discomfort in the face of causing someone else's anxiety, some adults spend a lifetime hiding from face-to-face, direct communication about behavior.

> **The skill of Benign Confrontation is an effective but challenging process. For many, confrontation is a scary prospect.**

Passive-aggressive individuals know this. They bank on it. In fact, they often select their adversaries based on this single criterion of who will be least likely to attempt to unmask the anger that they so desperately want to keep hidden. The bad news for those who shy away from confrontation is that without directly addressing passive-aggressive behavior, the pattern will be played out against them again and again. While the eight skills listed in Chapter 11 are highly effective from situation to situation, their impact rarely extends beyond the specific event. For lasting results and real behavioral change, Benign Confrontation of passive-aggressive behavior is necessary.

The good news is that Benign Confrontation is nothing to be afraid of! It is not an in-your-face, anger-inspiring, make-them-admit-what-they-did kind of authoritarian tactic but rather a quiet and reflective verbal intervention skill in which the adult gently but openly shares his or her thoughts about a person's behavior and unexpressed anger. It is based on the decision not to silently accept the person's manipulative and controlling behavior any longer.

The six-step process of Benign Confrontation of passive-aggressive behavior will equip you with skills to unmask the hidden anger of a passive-aggressive person and help that person gain insight into the destructive nature of his or her behavioral pattern. Rather than breaking the person down, this nontraditional confrontation approach builds the person up by strengthening the relationship, increasing self-awareness, and affirming areas of competence.

The Six Steps of Benign Confrontation

Benign Confrontation is the only technique we have found to be successful in changing the behavior of passive-aggressive persons. At its core, it works by identifying underlying anger. While a passive-aggressive person directs his or her cunning and effort into hiding anger and getting others to express it through their out-of-control behaviors, Benign Confrontation helps put the responsibility for the thoughts, feelings, and behaviors squarely back in the hands of the passive-aggressive person.

While Benign Confrontation has a powerful impact on the passive-aggressive individual, it is equally influential as a tool for an adult dealing with a passive-aggressive child, student, spouse, or coworker. Instead of getting caught up in frustrating arguments, endless conflict cycles, and relationship-damaging wars of words, the step-by-step process of Benign Confrontation gives the adult a road map for conflict navigation and hidden anger management. Whereas a final drip of passive-aggressive behavior customarily floods reactions and freezes up effective responses, Benign Confrontation allows an adult to maintain control of his or her emotions because of the adult's increased awareness of the dynamics taking place. The step-by-step approach helps the adult recall—even in the heat of the moment—where he or she is in the process with a passive-aggressive person and where to go next. The following is an outline of the steps of Benign Confrontation.

Step 1: Recognize the Patterns of Passive-Aggressive Behavior

The first two steps in the process of Benign Confrontation require proficiency in managing our own responses to passive-aggressive behavior. The very first thing one must do to effectively confront passive-aggressive behavior is to see beyond the sugarcoating and recognize the hostility that lies beneath. Keep in mind that passive-aggressive people have developed their personality styles over many years and that keeping their anger under wraps is an important priority for them. Being able to recognize the warning signs of passive aggression is very different from getting a person to admit that he or she has acted passive aggressively. It is a goal unto itself. Step 1 requires the adult to do the following:

> The very first thing one must do to effectively confront passive-aggressive behavior is to see beyond the sugarcoating and recognize the hostility that lies beneath.

A. Be able to recognize passive-aggressive behaviors as they are acted out (see Table 11.1).

B. Know the five levels of passive aggression (see Chapter 4).

Step 2: Refuse to Engage in the Passive-Aggressive Conflict Cycle

The passive-aggressive person not only masters concealing his or her anger but is also expert at getting an unsuspecting adult to act it out by entangling the adult in no-win power struggles. The second step in the process of Benign Confrontation is for the adult to refuse to engage in these passive-aggressive conflict cycles. In this way, the adult behaves unpredictably. For the passive-aggressive children, students, spouses, or coworkers accustomed to getting adults to act out their hidden anger, the adult who stops the Passive-Aggressive Conflict Cycle sends the message that he or she is different and that the passive-aggressive person will therefore have to relate to the adult on a different level. Step 2 requires the adult to do the following:

> The passive-aggressive person not only masters concealing her anger but is also expert at getting an unsuspecting adult to act it out by entangling the adult in no-win power struggles.

A. Acknowledge how frustrating it is to live, teach, and work with a person who is chronically passive aggressive.

B. Use self-talk strategies such as, "He is being passive aggressive, and I will not participate in his routine."

C. Replace counter–passive-aggressive "you" messages with assertive "I" statements.

D. Discontinue any reinforcement of passive-aggressive behavior.

Step 3: Affirm the Anger

This powerful step—affirming the anger—is where the adult turns the corner from the management of his own responses to the Benign Confrontation of the passive-aggressive behavior. It starts, logically, with an affirmation of the existence of the passive-aggressive person's underlying anger. The adult's acknowledgment of the person's anger will be unexpected; it is likely that the person has spent most of his or her life guarding and disguising this emotion and has never had anyone name it so plainly. Although the impact of this exposure will be profound, the façade of the angry smile will not likely be dropped right away. It is important for the adult to anticipate this and to know that the "admission of anger" is not the goal of Benign Confrontation. When the passive-aggressive person is shaken by the adult's unmasking of his or her anger, the person's self-protective instincts will engage, and he or she will use various defense mechanisms to recover his or her anger and redouble his or her efforts at concealment. This is an expected part of the process. Step 3 requires the adult to do the following:

A. Briefly recount the pertinent events leading up to the incident in which the person behaved passive aggressively.

B. Share a thought with the passive-aggressive person about the hidden anger that motivated his or her behavior ("It seems to me that the issue is that you are upset with me for making this request").

C. State that a difficulty in the relationship is the passive-aggressive person's reluctance to talk about his or her anger.

D. Keep in mind that this is neither an in-your-face retelling of events nor a critical rant but rather a quiet, reflective skill of *sharing a thought*. Benign Confrontation is the skill of gently dropping a pebble of a new idea into the passive-aggressive person's static pool of hostile thoughts.

> Benign Confrontation is the skill of gently dropping a pebble of a new idea into the passive-aggressive person's static pool of hostile thoughts.

Step 4: Manage the Denial

The goal of Benign Confrontation is to make overt the anger that has been covert, stuffed inside, and kept secret for so long. Expect that once this has been done in Step 3, the passive-aggressive person will deny the role that anger plays in the dynamic being discussed. The person typically uses a series of rationalizations to justify his or her actions, such as the following:

- "I forgot."

- "I didn't hear you."

- "I didn't know you wanted it done today."

- "No, I'm not angry. Why would you say this?"

When the person denies the role that his or her anger plays in the relationship or claims that he or she has been misunderstood, the adult should verbally accept the defenses for the time being, with a response such as, "Okay! It was just a thought I wanted to share with you." Following are two guidelines for managing a passive-aggressive person's denial of anger in Benign Confrontation:

1. Do not argue or correct the person's denial and rationalizations at this time, but rather quietly back away from further discussion.

2. Leave the person with the thought that you are aware that there are some feelings of anger behind his or her behavior.

The advantage of Benign Confrontation is the comfort of not having to justify or defend the stated observations about the person's underlying anger. By simply sharing with the person the awareness of his or her covert anger, the adult sends a bold and powerful message that the passive-aggressive behavior cannot continue and the relationship needs to change.

The effectiveness of Benign Confrontation begins after the person's initial defense of the shared observations of his or her covert anger. Though the person may deny it verbally, the person knows that his or her anger is not a secret anymore. Like a pebble dropped into a pool, the

> By sharing an awareness of the person's covert anger, the adult sends a bold and powerful message that the passive-aggressive behavior cannot continue and the relationship needs to change.

ripple effect of Benign Confrontation goes beyond the person's initial surprise that you have identified his or her underlying anger. Your revelation also takes away the secondary pleasure the person receives from being passive aggressive. Most important, the passive-aggressive person knows that his or her emotional mask has been lifted, and the door has been opened for future discussion about his or her underlying anger.

Step 5: Revisit the Thought

Benign Confrontation is not a once-and-done cure for passive-aggressive behavior but is rather an approach whose best results come from repetition. In the moment, the adult does not have to justify or defend his or her shared thoughts about a passive-aggressive person's behavior, because another moment will inevitably come and the adult's point will be best made by revisiting the thought at that time. For example, in Step 5, a wife might say to her husband,

> "I just had a thought I want to share with you. What just happened between us reminded me of a problem we had last week. Remember when I mentioned I thought you were angry at me? Well, this incident seems similar to that one. What do you think?"

The wife does not argue the point from here but rather leaves her husband with this thought to reverberate in his mind. Passive-aggressive individuals are usually quite intelligent, and though they may resist behavioral change, they are still likely to comprehend the point. Therefore, the next time the wife observes an example of passive-aggressive behavior from her husband, she may be able to simply say, "Guess what I am going to say about this behavior?" or "What do you think I am going to say next?"

The husband's typical answer is, "You probably are going to talk about my anger." This statement is an important acknowledgment of the change in the relationship. He knows he cannot hide behind the denial or rationalization (e.g., by saying, "I'm not mad," "I didn't hear you," or "I didn't understand what you wanted"). Also, he is no longer getting secondary pleasure from passive-aggressive behavior and now considers Benign Confrontation as an exposing, anxiety-provoking experience he wants to avoid. The husband faces two choices: to change the passive-aggressive behavior or to be benignly confronted by his wife again and again.

Step 6: Identify Areas of Competence

The final step in approaching a passive-aggressive person is a maintenance and relationship-building strategy. It is a move that need not be played immediately in the sequence, but it is important in motivating the passive-aggressive person toward change. When the adult who benignly confronts the passive-aggressive behavior is also able to identify and communicate areas of competence within the *person*, he or she succeeds in conveying the all-important message that the person is worthy and that behavioral change will be worthwhile.

We've used many terms throughout this text to convey the emotion that passive-aggressive people seek to hide—anger, hate, rage, hostility. No matter what the term or the degree of feeling, each is lessened every time the passive-aggressive person feels heard, understood, accepted, and competent. The six-step process of Benign Confrontation affords children, students, spouses, and coworkers the dignity of looking beyond their behaviors and seeking to understand the thoughts and feelings that simmer beneath.

The Key to a Successful Benign Confrontation

The key to a successful Benign Confrontation is to know when to speak and when to use silence. Remember that it only takes a spark to get a fire going. The most effective Benign Confrontations of passive-aggressive behavior are those that share a thought—that light the flame—and then leave the child, student, spouse, or coworker to consider, ponder, open his or her eyes, and feel the heat of the light that has been shed on that person's behaviors.

Benign Confrontation is not an in-your-face tactic when it comes to sharing thoughts, and neither should it shine a "flashlight" in the passive-aggressive person's eyes to try to "make" the person see his or her hidden anger. The biggest mistake adults make when addressing passive-aggressive behavior is to go overboard with their confrontation and to continue to drive home their thoughts over and over again in the moment. It's as if the adult is so struck by his own insight and newfound ability to correctly identify passive-aggressive behavior that he or she can't help but point it out from every angle.

Doing so, of course, pushes the passive-aggressive person's back into a corner and elicits the response that he or she is best known for: more passive aggression. Whether it be more intense denial, claims of victimhood, or even an insincere apology that gets the adult off of the person's back for the moment, the passive-aggressive person will respond unfavorably to this sort of challenge and will be more likely to resist the adult's shared thoughts in the future.

Example of Benign Confrontation

At School: Temporary Compliance

The following example of a passive-aggressive 12-year-old and her teacher demonstrates how Benign Confrontation can be used successfully with a student who displays Level 1 passive-aggressive behavior.

"Put the cards in the box, please"

Sarah is a smart, attractive 12-year-old who attends an alternative school. She is described as "delightful" whenever she is in control of an activity. When she feels she does not have control over a situation, however, her behaviors become manipulative and passive aggressive.

In this situation, Sarah was involved in a remedial writing lesson. She was asked by her teacher to stop her activity and put the cards from her writing lesson in a box so they could begin her math lesson. The box was right in front of Sarah. Sarah didn't respond to the teacher's first directive, so the teacher asked again. Sarah didn't respond to the second, third, or fourth requests, either. Each time she spoke her request, the teacher's voice rose by a few decibels. By the fifth request, the teacher was aware that Sarah heard her but was being silently oppositional. The teacher simultaneously gave herself this message: "This is a reasonable request and this girl is not going to win. There's no way I'm going to back down. She will put the cards in the box!" Already, the Passive-Aggressive Conflict Cycle was in full swing.

Sarah was clearly angry on the inside but smiled and looked pleasantly confused on the outside. She kept this up for the next 20 minutes without saying a word. The teacher was mirroring Sarah's behavior. She was angry on the inside but being sweet on the outside by repeating, "Please, put the cards in the box! You can put the cards away." Finally, "Put the cards away, Sarah!"

Benign Confrontation provides the teacher with a framework for responding effectively to passive aggression. The following sections describe this six-step approach.

Step 1: Recognize the Patterns of Passive-Aggressive Behavior

In this first step, the teacher should recognize Sarah's silent opposition as Level 1 passive aggression. Sarah appears to not hear the request, but smiles. She pretends deafness!

Step 2: Refuse to Engage in the Passive-Aggressive Conflict Cycle

In this step, the teacher should strive to control her counter–passive-aggressive feelings toward Sarah. After the second request to put the cards away, the teacher should have identified Sarah's behavior as passive aggressive and said to herself, "Sarah is being passive aggressive, and I will not participate in her strategy."

Step 3: Affirm the Anger

In Step 3, the teacher should share with Sarah her thoughts about the girl's underlying anger. The teacher should say calmly,

"Sarah, let's stop. I have a thought I want to share with you. I asked you to put away the cards, and you pretended not to hear me. I know I speak clearly, and other students can hear me easily. What I have to figure out is why, at this particular time, you are choosing not to hear me and follow my reasonable request."

If Sarah does not respond, the teacher should continue:

"My guess is that a part of you may be upset with me. You probably would prefer to continue to write than to do math right now. If so, we need to talk about your anger and stop pretending you can't hear me. Sarah, the difficulty we are having right now is not about the cards. We can forget about the cards and who puts them away. What is happening between us right now is important. Perhaps, we may have discovered a pattern of behavior you use when you are angry. Perhaps, when I ask you to do something you think is not fair or pleasurable, you act as if you don't hear me. Sarah, you are a smart student, so let me hear what you think about this situation."

Step 4: Manage the Denial

After this Benign Confrontation, which exposes Sarah's hidden anger, Sarah's first response is to refuse to talk or to deny it. At this time, the teacher should back off and not persist. The scenario would likely play out in the following way:

SARAH: (*Refuses to discuss the incident*)

TEACHER: It is difficult to talk about personal issues, but I want you to think about it.

SARAH: There is no problem here. I don't know what you're talking about. I'm not angry.

TEACHER: I'm glad you believe this is not a problem. In other words, if I ask you to do something like put the cards away, you will be willing to do it?

SARAH: (*Nods in agreement*)

Then, once again, the teacher should ask Sarah to put the cards in the box. A new level of insight will have developed between Sarah and her teacher. This process of Benign Confrontation will change the way Sarah and her teacher think about each other in the future. Sarah's passive-aggressive behavior is no longer a secret and effective technique of getting back at the adults in her life.

Step 5: Revisit the Thought

Each time the teacher identifies a clear example of Sarah's passive-aggressive behavior, the teacher should use Benign Confrontation to identify Sarah's underlying anger. The day after the cards-in-the-box-incident, Sarah nods her head at the teacher that she will clean up her art supplies, but she continues to paint long after the request is made. The teacher should revisit the thought from the previous day by saying the following:

"Sarah, I have a thought about what is happening here right now. Remember yesterday when I shared that I thought you were angry over our writing lesson ending and having to begin math? Your not cleaning up your paint reminds me of yesterday's situation, and I am wondering if this is your way of letting me know that you are angry again. What do you think?"

Step 6: Identify Areas of Competence

Though the moments immediately following a Benign Confrontation should be reserved for some calculated, intentional silence in which the passive-aggressive person is left to consider the thoughts shared by the adult, there should be a follow-up time in which the teacher works to build the relationship with Sarah. By identifying genuine areas of competence in Sarah, the teacher will show that although the passive-aggressive behavior is not functional in the relationship, the relationship itself is worthwhile.

In this scenario, because the teacher is aware that Sarah is "delightful" when she is in control of a situation, it might be to her advantage to give Sarah control over specific tasks in the classroom. The more Sarah can feel powerful in constructive ways, the less she may need to control through destructive passive aggression. The following are examples of areas of competence for Sarah:

- making her the "class timekeeper," whose job it is to alert the teacher when an allotted amount of time for an activity or lesson has passed

- putting her in charge of collecting the card boxes when Reading is over

- giving her a daily Lesson Checklist so that she can mark off each subject as she completes it

The specific competency area is not as important as the sheer act of reaching out to Sarah as a means of shrinking her hostility and increasing her motivation to relate on a new, more emotionally honest level.

A Final Note on Benign Confrontation

There is one last important angle to the concept of the Benign Confrontation of passive-aggressive behavior. While we have described in detail how to confront hidden anger and encourage its open, honest, direct expression, the critical next step for the confronting adult is the willingness to *receive* anger. Though a detailed exploration of this subtopic is beyond the scope of this book, it is worth a brief mention here: If you are going to guide a passive-aggressive person to be more direct and open with their anger, then you also must be willing to receive their anger. For many people, this is truly difficult. For lasting change to take hold for the passive-aggressive person, he or she must know that the assertive expression of his or her anger will be tolerated, accepted, honored, and even welcomed.

> If you are going to guide a passive-aggressive person to be more direct and open with his anger, then you also must be willing to receive his anger.

Summary

There is a phrase often used in recovery treatment that says, "We are as sick as our secrets." This saying rings true for passive aggression as well. As long as anger remains hidden, it can't be changed. The goal of Benign Confrontation for passive-aggressive persons is to affirm their anger; only by acknowledging its existence can a passive-aggressive person be set on a path toward developing insight into the self-defeating pattern and then choosing to change.

In this chapter, we have detailed the six steps for the Benign Confrontation of passive-aggressive behavior:

Step 1: Recognize the patterns of passive-aggressive behavior

Step 2: Refuse to engage in the Passive-Aggressive Conflict Cycle

Step 3: Affirm the anger

Step 4: Manage the denial

Step 5: Revisit the thought

Step 6: Identify areas of competence

We have provided a guided example for confronting Level 1 passive-aggressive behavior in school, following each of the six steps. In the Appendix, you will find three additional examples that demonstrate Benign Confrontation at Levels 2 through 4 in the home, in close adult relationships, and in the workplace. These long-term intervention skills for changing passive-aggressive behavior combined with the eight short-term skills for changing responses to passive aggression combine to form a comprehensive approach to passive-aggressive behavior at all levels, across all ages.

Closing

We hope that after reading this book you find the study of passive aggression to be an exciting psychological adventure that changes the way you think, feel, and behave toward a passive-aggressive person. You now understand the hidden mystery of passive aggression and can avoid being lured into a passive-aggressive conflict. You have the knowledge to change your responses to passive-aggressive behavior and have learned an effective intervention skill called Benign Confrontation. As you practice these skills, you will become more comfortable and confident talking about the unexpressed anger in your relationships. The psychology of passive aggression provides the knowledge and skills to live, teach, and work with a person who is passive aggressive in a different and more satisfying way . . . assuming you don't procrastinate.

References

American Psychiatric Association. (1952). *Diagnostic and statistical manual of mental disorders.* Washington, DC: Author.

American Psychiatric Association. (1968). *Diagnostic and statistical manual of mental disorders* (2nd ed.). Washington, DC: Author.

American Psychiatric Association. (1980). *Diagnostic and statistical manual of mental disorders* (3rd ed.). Washington, DC: Author.

American Psychiatric Association. (1994). *Diagnostic and statistical manual of mental disorders* (4th ed.). Washington, DC: Author.

American Psychiatric Association. (2000). *Diagnostic and statistical manual of mental disorders* (4th ed., text rev.). Washington, DC: Author.

Brown, P. B. (2005, October 22). *The passive aggressive workplace.* Retrieved February 10, 2008, from http://www.nytimes.com/2005/10/22/business/22offline.html?partner=rss nyt&emc=rss&pagewanted=print

Burns, D. (1991). *Feeling good.* New York: Avon Books.

Carey, B. (2004, November 16). *Oh, fine, you're right. I'm passive aggressive.* Retrieved February 10, 2008, from http://www.nytimes.com/2004/11/16/health/psychology/16pass.html?_r=1&oref=slogin

Childhelp. (n.d.). *National child abuse statistics.* Retrieved July 7, 2008, from http://www.childhelp.org/resources/learning-center/statistics

Ginott, G. H. (1972). *Between teacher and child.* New York: Collier's Books.

Kantor, M. (2002). *Passive-aggression: A guide for the therapist, the patient and the victim.* Westport, CT: Praeger.

Long, N. J. (2007). The Conflict Cycle Paradigm: How troubled students get teachers out of control. In N. J. Long, W. C. Morse, F. A. Fecser, & R. G. Newman (Eds.), *Conflict in the Classroom* (pp. 325–349). Austin, TX: PRO-ED.

Long, J., & Long, N. J. (1996). Understanding and managing the passive aggressive student. In N. J. Long & W. Morse (Eds.), *Conflict in the classroom* (5th ed., pp. 352–361). Austin, TX: PRO-ED.

Long, N. J. (1996). The conflict cycle paradigm on how troubled students get teachers out of control. In N. J. Long & W. Morse (Eds.), *Conflict in the classroom* (5th ed., pp. 244–264). Austin, TX: PRO-ED.

Long, N. J. (1998, October). *The angry smile: Understanding and managing passive aggressive behavior of students and staff.* Paper presented at the Conflict Cycle Paradigm, KidsPeace National Center for Kids in Crisis, 16th National Conference, Allendale, PA.

Long, N. J., & Newman, R. (1961, July). *The teacher's handling of children in conflict.* Bloomington: Indiana University, School of Education.

Marquoit, J. (2004, September 22). Reclaiming the passive-aggressive youth. *Reclaiming Children and Youth: The Journal of Strength-Based Interventions, 13*(3), 177.

Murphy, T., & Oberlin, L. H. (2005). *Overcoming passive aggression: How to stop hidden anger from spoiling your relationships, career, and happiness.* New York: Marlowe.

Namka, L. (1998). *The boomerang relationship: Passivity, irresponsibility and resulting partner anger.* Retrieved February 13, 2008, from http://www.angriesout.com/couples8.htm

Philips, M. (2008, February 11). I need a hit man. Now. *Newsweek Magazine,* p. 53.

Rosenfeld, M. (1997, November 10). Daddy severest. *Washington Post,* p. B1.

Sandberg, J. (2005, November 27). *Passive aggression may be the perfect office crime.* Retrieved February 11, 2008, from http://findarticles.com/p/articles/mi_qn4188/is_20051127/ai_n15874397

Silver, L. (1992). *Dr. Larry Silver's advice to parents on attention-deficit hyperactivity disorder.* Washington, DC: American Psychiatric Press.

Smith, S. (1992). *Succeeding against the odds.* Los Angeles: Jeremy P. Tarcher.

Unterberg, M. P. (2003, October 15). *Personality disorders in the workplace: The underachieving, compliant employee.* Retrieved February 10, 2008, from http://managedhealthcareexecutive.modernmedicine.com/mhe/Psychology/Personality-Disorders-in-the-Workplace-The-Underac/ArticleStandard/Article/detail/134268

Wetzler, S. (1992a). *Living with the passive aggressive man: Coping with hidden aggression—from bedroom to boardroom.* New York: Simon & Schuster.

Wetzler, S. (1992b, October 12). Sugarcoated hostility. *Newsweek Magazine,* p. 14.

Additional Examples of Benign Confrontation

In Close Adult Relationships: Intentional Inefficiency

This example revisits the scenario of Richard and Kelly's Passive-Aggressive Conflict Cycle over putting their daughter to bed at night, which was first examined in Chapter 3. As we rewind the scene a bit, we demonstrate how Benign Confrontation can be used successfully with a spouse who displays Level 2 passive-aggressive behavior.

Step 1: Recognize the Patterns of Passive-Aggressive Behavior

Once Kelly is aware of typical patterns of passive-aggressive behavior, she can recognize that her husband's unspoken reluctance to give up his evening free time is being expressed through the intentional undoing of an established bedtime routine.

Step 2: Refuse to Engage in the Passive-Aggressive Conflict Cycle

While Kelly waits downstairs for Richard to put Hayley to bed, she should manage her rising anger through self-talk strategies, such as, "Richard didn't want to put Hayley to bed tonight. Rather than telling me in words, he is showing me through this passive-aggressive behavior. I will not allow myself to get caught up in a no-win Passive-Aggressive Conflict Cycle here."

Step 3: Affirm the Anger

When Richard returns downstairs, Kelly should share her thoughts about his underlying anger.

KELLY: I have a thought I'd like to share with you. I asked you to put Hayley to bed tonight. You agreed without hesitation, and I appreciated that. When you spent over an hour upstairs and played instead of settling her down, her bedtime routine was disrupted. I know I have explained how important the routine is, so what I have to figure out is why, at this particular time, you decided to change it.

RICHARD: We were just having some fun.

KELLY: I just can't help but think that there is more to it than that. I am wondering if a part of you may be upset with me for having asked you to put Hayley to bed when what you really wanted to do was relax downstairs. Perhaps you went overboard with the fun and so tomorrow night I would be less likely to ask you to take charge of bedtime again. This really isn't about the time Hayley goes to sleep, but more about what is happening between us right now.

Step 4: Manage the Denial

No matter how nonthreatening the language Kelly chooses (*Is it possible that . . . My sense is that . . . I am wondering if . . .*) it is almost certain that Richard will cling to his story that he and his daughter were just enjoying their time together. If Kelly were to push harder, Richard would become more defensive and would likely play the role of fun-father victim to the overly rigid mother. If she were to use angry "you" messages or seek revenge in a counter–passive-aggressive way, she would reinforce his original passive aggression. Kelly will be best served by leaving Richard with the thought, as in the following:

RICHARD: I don't know what you are talking about. I got her to sleep, like you asked. I haven't spent time with her all day. Lighten up!

KELLY: Okay. It was just a thought I wanted to share with you.

Step 5: Revisit the Thought

The next time Kelly asks Richard to put Hayley to bed (or share a different household responsibility), it will be essential for her to modify her own behavior, as a preventative response to her husband's anticipated passive-aggressive behavior. Kelly should make it a habit to communicate clear expectations any time she makes a request of Richard.

Though this skill (described in Chapter 11) will go a long way in preventing predictable passive aggression, similar situations will inevitably arise that relate to household or parenting responsibilities. When they do, Kelly should remind Richard of the thoughts she shared after the bedtime incident:

Richard, I have a thought about what is going on here. This situation feels a lot like the one we had last week when I asked you to put Hayley to bed. I shared with you then that I thought you might have been angry at me. I am wondering if the same thing might be going on right now.

Step 6: Identify Areas of Competence

At a later point, it will be worthwhile for Kelly to affirm for Richard the strength of his bond with Hayley and ways that he might enjoy their time together. By building in free time for Richard at home, he may feel more open to sharing parental responsibilities. When she acknowledges the household responsibilities that he does well, Kelly can chip away at the hostility Richard feels at having his "relaxation" time eroded. In partnership with the Benign Confrontation of unacceptable passive-aggressive behavior, the overall relationship is nurtured and strengthened. This, in turn, defuses some of the angry feelings that would otherwise fuel the next Passive-Aggressive Conflict Cycle.

At Work: Letting a Problem Escalate

To demonstrate the effectiveness of Benign Confrontation in very delicate relationships, such as between an employee and a supervisor, we revisit the following Level 3 scenario from Chapter 8:

> A supervisor knows that an employee has not been informed of critical updates before a presentation to the board of directors. Intimidated by her competence and "rising star" quality, he allows her to go on with the presentation and appear foolish in front of the decision makers.

Step 1: Recognize the Patterns of Passive-Aggressive Behavior

Amidst the professional humiliation and embarrassment of the flubbed presentation, it may be an emotional challenge for the employee to recognize that what occurred was the result of a passive-aggressive dynamic between her and her supervisor. This ability to see the pattern is essential for her to respond effectively.

Step 2: Refuse to Engage in the Passive-Aggressive Conflict Cycle

Though the emotions that follow the presentation may be overwhelming, the employee needs to manage them through self-talk strategies, such as,

> "My boss knew that the new numbers had been reported. He didn't pass on the information to me because he didn't want me to appear competent in front of the board members. He is showing his resentment of my work through his passive-aggressive behavior. I will not allow myself to appear even more foolish by acting out his hostility."

Step 3: Affirm the Anger

Confronting a superior at work can be challenging even with the most overt of their actions. When it comes to passive-aggressive behaviors that will predictably be denied, the challenge is even greater. Yet, for this employee to ensure that her entire career path is not sabotaged and the company's productivity is not thwarted, it is essential that she assert her thoughts.

EMPLOYEE: I have a thought I'd like to share with you. I did not have access to the financial updates prior to my presentation to the board. I know now that the numbers were available and that you had them in your possession at the meeting. What I am wondering is why you did not share the information with me.

SUPERVISOR: I thought you saw the report.

EMPLOYEE: I was not aware that the numbers were even available. I do not have access to the reports. I always wait for you to pass them on to me. In this case, the information was not shared, so the figures I presented to the board were out of date. I appeared to be uninformed. I can't help but wonder if there is a reason you did not pass on the information to me before the meeting. If there is something that I did that was upsetting, please tell me.

Step 4: Manage the Denial

Again, it is highly unlikely that a supervisor with a pattern of passive-aggressive behavior would choose this moment to be emotionally honest and admit to his actions. He will be affected by the employee's nonaccusatory candor—perhaps expecting her to either rant at him or silently accept her humiliation—but he will continue to guard his emotion and verbally deny anger.

SUPERVISOR: I'm not angry with you. I must have just forgotten to give you a copy of the numbers. It should have been your responsibility to check with me before the presentation.

EMPLOYEE: It was just a thought I had. Thank you for letting me express my concern. I should have checked with you before the meeting. This has been a learning experience for me.

Step 5: Revisit the Thought

This type of situation is especially delicate because it goes against the grain of so many workplace hierarchies for an employee to confront a supervisor. This underscores why Benign Confrontation is such an effective tool. Without using loud, accusatory, professionally inappropriate tactics, even someone with less "power" in a dynamic can effectively assert his or her thoughts and observations about particular behavior. Because a supervisor in a work setting is generally not accustomed to being challenged by his or her supervisees, Benign Confrontation stands out. Its distinctness from more commonly employed aggressive or passive responses from supervisees makes Benign Confrontation particularly effective.

Though we may assume this supervisor will receive a clear message from the employee, it remains inevitable that the employee will need to maintain communication on this level in the future. Each time she observes his passive-aggressive tactics, she should consider revisiting the thoughts she shared after the presentation.

Step 6: Identify Areas of Competence

Although supervisors typically look for areas of competence in their staff, in this scenario, it will be in the employee's best interests to find a way to work with her boss rather than waiting for him to work against her. Where the employee can find ways to gain recognition for both her and her boss, she will shrink his hostility at her successes and defuse the anger that lies beneath his passive-aggressive office crimes.

At Home: Hidden but Conscious Revenge

In this final example, we explore how Benign Confrontation works against the serious and troubling Level 4 form of passive-aggressive behavior. In this scenario, an adolescent is accused by her stepfather of taking money from his wallet.

Step 1: Recognize the Patterns of Passive-Aggressive Behavior

When the stepfather realizes that four 20-dollar bills are missing from his wallet, he immediately suspects that his adolescent stepdaughter has taken them. His hunch is confirmed by his 6-year-old son, Chris, who says he saw his half-sister take money out of the wallet. At first, the stepfather sees the situation as a crime. Upon further reflection, he recognizes the theft as part of a larger pattern of anger, in which his stepdaughter acts out her hidden hostility toward his presence in the family.

Step 2: Refuse to Engage in the Passive-Aggressive Conflict Cycle

Given their conflictual relationship, it would be easy for this incident to become a clash of criminal accusations, denial, threats of legal repercussions, and cries of victimhood. What would be more difficult would be to address the intense and deeply felt emotions that are driving the stepdaughter's passive aggression. Though engaging in a passive-aggressive conflict cycle would, in the short term, be easier than addressing the child's raw, buried emotion, the long-term benefit to addressing her hidden anger and ending the cycle of conflict could make all the difference in the quality of the family's life.

Step 3: Affirm the Anger

The stepfather should calmly share his thoughts about his stepdaughter's underlying anger.

STEPFATHER: I have a problem I want to share with you. I noticed that four 20-dollar bills were missing from my wallet. One of the kids mentioned seeing you take something out of my wallet earlier.

STEPDAUGHTER: I was just borrowing the money for a pair of cleats I need for soccer. I was going to write you a note. I just forgot.

STEPFATHER: I usually give you what you need to pay for your sports and activities. The problem I am having is that you did not ask me for the money, but went into my wallet. If you take something of mine without my knowing, that's not borrowing. It is stealing.

STEPDAUGHTER: (*Interrupts*) I wasn't stealing it!

STEPFATHER: The problem we are having right now is perhaps about something much more important than money. I think you might be feeling angry with me for being a part of your family's life. If so, we need to talk about it rather than having you act in ways that could hurt us both. My guess is that your taking the money wasn't actually about the money or shoes or buying anything, but rather your way of sending me the message that you are angry about our relationship. What do you think?

Step 4: Manage the Denial

STEPDAUGHTER: I'm not mad at you. I don't really care about you one way or the other. I just needed $75 and you weren't around for me to ask, so I took it.

STEPFATHER: You know, I'm wrong a lot and I could be way off on this one too, but it was just something I had been noticing and I wanted you to know my thoughts about it.

In his words, the stepfather allows the stepdaughter to "save face" with his "I could be wrong" phrasing. Yet the point that he is aware of her hidden anger has still been communicated and the intended message has been irrevocably sent.

Step 5: Revisit the Thought

The next time the stepfather becomes aware of other passive-aggressive behaviors by his stepdaughter at any level, he must share his thoughts again. Because her passive aggression has escalated to a criminal level, it will be critical for every family member's sake that her passive-aggressive behavior be benignly confronted at every turn. Also, as the more serious Level 4 offenses are committed, the stepfather will have to use the skills discussed in Chapter 11, setting very clear expectations, taking away the gratification she receives from her passive aggression, and allowing natural consequences to occur.

Step 6: Identify Areas of Competence

Through the process of Benign Confrontation, the stepfather communicates that he is aware of his stepdaughter's underlying anger. This "I know that you know" and "I know that you know that I know" understanding can strengthen their relationship and open the doors for greater honesty. It will be important for the relationship to be nurtured across all areas so that honest communication can be maintained and so that the stepdaughter's hostility will be decreased and the need for passive-aggressive forms of emotional expression will be diminished.

About the Authors

Dr. Jody E. Long is a licensed school psychologist who served for many years in the District of Columbia school system. She received her PhD in counseling psychology from the American University and served as coordinator of the American University–Rose School Program. She has coauthored *Conflict in College* as well as several professional articles on adolescence. Currently, she serves on the boards of directors of the Life Space Crisis Intervention Institute, the Maryland Symphony Orchestra, and the Washington County Museum of Fine Arts in Hagerstown, MD. Her avocations include Renaissance art and interior design. She and her husband Nicholas have five children and six grandchildren.

Dr. Nicholas J. Long is a national leader in teaching and programming for emotionally disturbed children and youth. He received his PhD from the University of Michigan in 1957 and has served on the faculty of Indiana University, Georgetown University, and the American University, where he is professor emeritus. A licensed clinical psychologist, he also served as executive director of the Hillcrest Children's Psychiatry Center in Washington, DC. He has co-authored *Conflict in the Classroom* (6th ed.) and *Life Space Intervention*. Currently he is president of the Life Space Crisis Intervention Institute.

Signe Whitson is a licensed social worker and program administrator for the Life Space Crisis Intervention Institute. She has worked as a therapist for severely emotionally disturbed adolescents and as a trainer for professionals. She has developed and delivered numerous training curricula around the country in areas related to child and adolescent mental health. She has served as an adjunct professor of psychology at Moravian University and Lehigh Carbon Community College and as an adjunct professor of social work at Marywood University's Graduate School of Social Work. She co-edited McGraw-Hill's 2002 *Annual Editions Online: Adolescent Psychology*.